RAMBLE

A Field Guide To The

U.S.A.

BY

ERIC PETERSON

speck press

denver

Copyright 2006 © Eric Peterson
Published by: speck press, speckpress.com

ISBN 1-933108-08-8, ISBN-13: 978-1-933108-08-7

See page 218 for photo credits
Maps courtesy of Microsoft® Streets & Trips 2006 with GPS Locator
www.microsoft.com/streets

This publication is provided for informational and educational purposes. The
information herein contained is true and complete to the best of our knowledge.

Book layout and design by CPG, corvuspublishinggroup.com

Printed and bound in China

Library of Congress Cataloging-in-Publication Data

Peterson, Eric, 1973-
 Ramble : a field guide to the U.S.A. / by Eric Peterson.
   p. cm.
 Includes index.
 ISBN-13: 978-1-933108-08-7 (pbk. : alk. paper)
 ISBN-10: 1-933108-08-8 (pbk. : alk. paper)
 1. United States--Description and travel. 2. Peterson, Eric, 1973---Travel--United
States. 3. United States--History, Local. 4. United States--Guidebooks. I. Title.

E169.Z83P4755 2006
917.304'93--dc22

                              2006003753

                        10 9 8 7 6 5 4 3 2 1

TO MY FAITHFUL MUTT **GIBLET**

1994–2006

**Thanks for staying home or coming along for the ride,
even though you had no choice.**

Acknowledgements

Many thanks to John and Vicki Peterson, Ingvald Grunder,
Larry Kellogg, Anna Dhody, Devon Manelski, Aaron and Jen Conway,
Brian Barnes, Jason Brooks, David Bailey,
Karlo Kitanovski and Grandma, Gladys Chase, Pampa and Mary,
the Gilmer family, Greg and Amy Feldman, Dave Koterwas,
Mark and Jean Stefani, Thomas Nygard, Tanya Rees, Pat Haight,
John Allen, Cliff Barnes, Linda Elliff, Derek Lawrence,
Susan Hill Newton, Margaret McCullough,
Bobby and Kendra Mandarich,
Mark McKitterick, Jaimie Smith, and Pan Smith.

CHAPTER 8 *Sin and Salvation*

CHAPTER 9 *The Midwest and the Northwoods*

CHAPTER 10 *American Sideshow* — 140

CHAPTER 11 *New England and the Northeast* — 154

INTRODUCTION

Rambling is nothing new. I'm not going to try and claim I invented it or perfected it. I'll even admit that I've done some of the stupidest shit in travel history, from locking myself on a San Francisco rooftop (with my dog) to getting lost in the industrial tundra of Gary, Indiana.

No, rambling is nothing new. Just ask Ramblin' Jack Elliot about it, or listen to "Ramblin' Man" or "Ramble On." But some ninety years before Zeppelin first charted, Edwin J. Stanley wrote an 1878 Yellowstone guidebook entitled *Rambles in Wonderland.* Clearly, rambling is something that's been a prime human endeavor for quite some time.

Stanley wrote about Yellowstone in a self-conscious tone, always humbling his abilities to put the park's natural marvels into words while maintaining a high note of condescension to his audience. A difficult balance, yes, but Stanley pulls it off without a hitch.

Consider how Stanley couches his description of Yellowstone's Upper Geyser Basin: "[N]ever did language seem more inadequate to the task, nor my efforts at pen-picturing so sadly felt, as I attempt a portrayal of the utterly indescribable wonders of the Upper Geyser Basin. I am tempted to throw away the pen in disgust."

Strong words. I've considered chucking my laptop against the wall when thoroughly disgusted with my own work, typically as I regurgitated trade rag drivel. But the inclination to throw away the pen in disgust is a recurring theme in travel writing, where the translation of experience into words, format, and editorial voice often results in something that reads, even to the writer, as if it were in a foreign tongue.

But I digress.

Writes Stanley on the topic of Yellowstone's Upper and Lower Falls: "This place is of great interest to the tourist, where he will be tempted to tarry long amid the wondrous grandeur and beauty of scenes which even the finest linguist must ever fail to describe and the most skillful artist despair of painting, the eye being the only medium through which a just conception of the surpassing beauty and sublimity of the place can be obtained."

A little verbose perhaps, but pretty much spot-on even today. I assume Mr. Stanley was being paid by the word. But again he casts doubt on his own ability to use words to effectively depict the scene.

Words and great writing, and great travel writing, only go so far. In the end, the best a writer can hope for is to spark the reader's curiosity to such an extent that he or she actually goes and visits the area described and experiences a similar sense of wonder.

Or, as Stanley puts it, "We find ourselves lost in contemplation, and the mind is completely overwhelmed as it tries to grapple with the momentous subjects presented."

Good point, Edwin J. That is the Zen of the Road. That is why we travel, why we drive all night on coffee and loud music, our right feet gaining a blister from the gas pedal as our asses lose all sense of feeling from the seat. For many of us, it is why we live.

Later in *Rambles*, Stanley describes his party's experience on the Grand Canyon of the Yellowstone's floor as … "feeling we were in the very antechamber of the great God of Nature, and that he was talking to us and teaching us lessons of his greatness, his grandeur and his glory, that human language must ever fail to express. A sense of the awful pervades the mind, and we almost felt that we were trespassing on sacred ground."

Which you surely were, Mr. Stanley. But ultimately no chunk of land is any more sacred than any other, and there's plenty of land to both share and carve out our own antechamber to the great God of Nature, whatever form he/she may take, a big blue elephant or a giant Kenny Rogers in the sky.

I stumbled upon Stanley's book in the early stages of *Ramble*, while working on a guidebook about Yellowstone for a major guidebook publisher. The Buffalo Bill Historical Center in Cody, Wyoming, had an exhibit covering art in Yellowstone that referred to *Rambles*. I hunted down esteemed (and remarkably funny) Yellowstone park historian Lee Whittlesey, who immediately recounted the book's author, its date of publication, and the fact that the author did indeed venture to the park to research the book.

I burned a callus onto my right index finger with a pencil in the library at the Heritage and Research Center the next afternoon, scribbling eight pages of Edwin's words onto a legal pad. As I typed them out that night in a creekside cabin with a woodburning stove and no bathroom, I couldn't agree more with his opinion, if not his writing style.

The whole thing reminds me that rambling is not only an inherently American activity, but something that is innately human. We want to wander around and see new things, grasping at the polar opposite of our own realities. We either suppress it or we indulge, we all go on a journey, and that is life.

In the end, there are only two kinds of stories: a person goes on a journey or a stranger comes to town. The road trip encompasses both, and, best of all, you're the protagonist every time.

CALIFORNIA

The balmy, misguided paradise of California—named after an imaginary archipelago in a fifteenth-century Spanish romance novel—is vacation heaven for some and hell on Earth for others. Sure, the beaches and theme parks and scenery are nice, but the traffic and smog and sprawl are anything but.

Regardless, the Golden State is still the ultimate road-trip destination. It's literally the end of the road—if for no other reason than the lack of dry land if you continue west. Then there's the possibility of the Big One, which would make dry land in California that much more scarce and expensive.

The highest peak in the lower forty-eight, Mount Whitney, is also here, but countless other mountains of rock and flesh have been removed by bulldozer and Botox and rebuilt out of concrete and silicone.

The weather—typically seventy degrees and sunny—attracts all sorts of professionals, especially stars (rock/pop, movie stars, and porn), the members of said stars' posses, and said stars' agents. The favorable climate also appeals to a wide range of addicts, criminals, and lunatics who do not like the cold.

This means people watching in California is no mere diversion—it's a full-time job. In Southern California, common specimens include disillusioned also-rans and strung-out never-weres; less common are the rich and famous, a group far outnumbered by the poor and desperate. Farther north, you'll find the country's stinkiest hippies and its richest geeks.

California is home to one of the most ethnically diverse populations on the planet. The suburbs have street signs in Vietnamese and other non-English languages as the kids continue to develop new indigenous languages (i. e., surfer dude and Valley girl) that have more to do with age than ethnic heritage.

CALIFORNIA (POP. 35,484,000)

- About a half-million detectable earthquakes shake California every year.

- California produces 17 million gallons of wine a year—about 34 gallons per seismic tremor, to help soothe the nerves.

- The name "California" dates back to *Las Sergas de Esplandian*, a 1510 romance novel by Garcia Ordonez de Montalvo. The sixteenth-century Spanish explorers who named the region were presumably big fans of the romance genre.

- Sierra Madre's Lavender Lady is the world's largest blooming plant, a wisteria vine with branches 500 feet long.

Money is just about everywhere in California, the only exception being where it's most needed. This is an economy so big and diverse it encompasses Disneyland and porn-makers in the San Fernando Valley, as well as the odd corporate entity that specializes in adult video featuring costumed dwarves.

Whether you're cruising for hookers on Hollywood Boulevard or trying to score weed in the Haight, California has something for everybody. Except, of course, the poor.

BIG THINGS AND OTHER ROAD ART

WORLD'S LARGEST THERMOMETER
I-15, EXIT 246
BAKER, CA

The heat in the California desert can be downright demoralizing. I guess it's always been that way; places get names like "Death Valley" for a reason.

The lowest spot in the Western Hemisphere—bottoming out at 282 feet below sea level—Death Valley saw its sizzle hit a North American record of 134 degrees Fahrenheit back on July 10, 1913.

About three-quarters of a century later, Willis Herron, one of the proprietors of the Bun Boy Restaurant in the parched little town of Baker, brainstormed for a way to kick-start the local economy and came up with a sixty-foot thermometer. Somebody mentioned that it should be 134 feet, in honor of that horrific day back in 1913. Herron was happy to oblige and refused to listen to his family's pleas for a beach house as he sunk $700,000 into the monster thermometer, lit with almost 5,000 bulbs on three sides to reflect the current temperature.

Easily the world's largest thermometer—and only seventeen feet shorter than the Statue of Liberty—Baker's claim to fame did indeed give the town's tourist trade a nice boost when it went up in 1991. It remains the best manmade photo op in the California desert.

Reading:

- *Dharma Bums*, Jack Kerouac
- *Cannery Row*, John Steinbeck
- *A Coney Island State of the Mind*, Lawrence Ferlinghetti

Viewing:

- *The Player*
- *Pulp Fiction*
- *Blade Runner*
- *Chinatown*

Listening:

- *Pet Sounds*, Beach Boys
- *Straight Outta Compton*, N. W. A.
- *L. A. Woman*, The Doors
- *California Uberalis*, Dead Kennedys

To-do Checklist:

- Impersonate the paparazzi
- Puke at Disneyland
- Puke in Oakland
- Leave your heart in San Francisco
- The desert, man

BUBBLEGUM ALLEY
700 BLOCK OF HIGUERA ST.
SAN LUIS OBISPO, CA

One of the downright grossest works of public art on the planet, Bubblegum Alley is exactly what it sounds like: an alley plastered over with gum chewed by thousands of mouths.

Since the 1960s, passersby have molded their own used Bazooka, Juicy Fruit, and Big Red onto a grimy collage of sticky bubblegum. Now entirely swathed in a layer of gum several sticks and a few balls thick, the alley's walls play host to truly nauseating abstract murals that would have even sickened Jackson Pollock.

Best (or possibly worst) of all, Bubblegum Alley is interactive. Nearby storefronts keep their gumball machines stocked with plenty of ammo.

"You get a very real notion of what it might be like to try and be creative in hell."

—Ira Hirsch on Bubblegum Alley

CABAZON DINOSAURS
ADJACENT TO I-10, MAIN ST. EXIT
CABAZON, CA
WWW.CABAZONDINOSAURS.COM

There's nothing that says, "I'm almost to Los Angeles," like the Cabazon Dinosaurs, the colossal *Tyrannosaurus rex* (Mr. Rex) and *Apatosaurus* (Ms. Dinny) sidling up to I-10 in the California desert. Famous for their cameo in *Pee Wee's Big Adventure*, Mr. Rex and Ms. Dinny are the work of the late Claude Bell, who worked on the twin dinos until his passing in 1989. Since then, Bell's work was first threatened with demolition and recently fell into the hands of a creationist concern who sell anti-evolution books and gifts right out of Ms. Dinny's prodigious belly.

WATTS TOWERS
1765 E. 107TH ST.
LOS ANGELES, CA
213-847-4646

Watts does not get the tourists it should. While most of L.A.'s visitors skip South Central in favor of Anaheim, they're missing out on a series of towering spires that put Sleeping Beauty's Castle to shame.

The Watts Towers are seventeen distinct structures crafted by Italian immigrant Simon Rodia between 1931 and 1955. The Towers, supported by a skeleton of steel pipes, are clad in a multihued mosaic of tile, broken pottery, seashells, glass shards, and other salvaged materials. The tallest measures ninety-nine feet, six inches. Like Florida's Coral Castle and Colorado's Bishop Castle, it's hard to fathom that this is all the work of just one man who shunned scaffolding, power equipment, bolts, and blueprints.

In 1955, Rodia picked up stakes and essentially abandoned his life's work. His shack burned down, leading the City of Los Angeles to condemn the property and order his sculptures razed. But a group of locals came together to save these masterpieces of folk art. Since then, they survived both the Watts Riots and the Northridge Earthquake. It looks like they're around for the long haul after all.

R. I. P.

HOLLYWOOD FOREVER CEMETERY
6000 SANTA MONICA BLVD.
LOS ANGELES, CA
WWW.CEMETERYSCREENINGS.COM

I took a swig off my beer and surveyed the scene. A thousand or so people were crowded onto a wide, open green next to a big, white building. It was a bustling outdoor party with picnics and pizzas and booze. It was Saturday night in the middle of a cemetery. The big, white building was about to serve as a screen for the movie *Carrie*.

"Who's buried here?" I asked a compatriot.

"Rudolf Valentino," came his answer. "Douglas Fairbanks. And the girl Fatty Arbuckle supposedly murdered."

I remarked that it was an unusually festive scene to see in a normally solemn and silent place like a graveyard.

"It's a party in their honor, the people who are buried here," said my friend. "I think they'd want us to be here, having a good time and enjoying life."

A few minutes later, *Carrie*'s opening locker room sequence began flickering on the structure in front of us. The crowd cheered. I leaned back and enjoyed the movie, the perfect film for that perfect moment in time.

Screenings are held Saturday nights in the summer.

COLMA

Just south of San Francisco
Colma, CA
650-997-8300
WWW.COLMA.CA.GOV

Starting with the gold-fueled population boom in 1849, San Francisco has had a tough time disposing of its dead. As more and more people lived in the city, more and more also died in the city. With real estate a scarce commodity, San Francisco's leaders banned the burial of dead bodies within city lines in 1902.

This policy paved the way for Colma. Founded in 1924, Colma is now home to a population of 1.5 million people, as the saying goes, but only 1,100 are breathing. Today, 73 percent of Colma's land area is cemetery land. There are sixteen cemeteries in town. Everybody who was anybody in San Francisco is buried here, including Joe

DiMaggio (Holy Cross Cemetery), Levi Strauss (Home of Peace Cemetery), Wyatt Earp (Hills of Eternity Memorial Park), William Randolph Hearst (Cypress Lawn Memorial Park), and self-proclaimed Emperor of the United States Joshua Norton (Woodlawn Memorial Park).

VICE

THE EMERALD TRIANGLE
HUMBOLDT, MENDOCINO, AND TRINITY COUNTIES
NORTH COAST, CA

The Emerald Triangle, comprised of the three Northern California counties of Humboldt, Mendocino, and Trinity, is named for the color of its chief cash crop: high-grade marijuana. The region is considered the largest producer of marijuana in the United States.

While the value of the region's ganja industry is not known, a Humboldt State University professor has been quoted estimating Humboldt County's weed industry alone at upwards of $500 million a year. Multiply that range by three and we're talking about a billion-dollar industry at minimum, an industry at least in the same general ballpark as Hollywood's modest movie trade.

The Emerald Triangle's weed economy was initially underpinned by a favorable climate and the large workforce of hippies in the general vicinity. Both of these factors have become less integral over time. Police choppers drove most of the growing indoors during the Reagan years, and peace-loving hippies have by and large been replaced by gun-toting capitalists. Trespassing is not recommended.

Based on an ingrained cultural tolerance for really good marijuana and an economy that depends on it, the Emerald Triangle is just about the closest thing to the Netherlands on American soil. Just be discrete.

"The cultivation of cannabis is widespread in Northern California, especially in the Emerald Triangle. The large-scale outdoor cultivation sites that dot the Emerald Triangle often use sophisticated irrigation systems to produce thousands of pounds of high-grade, high-demand marijuana annually."

—Department of Justice website

"Lately even local politicians and police seem to have made their peace with the drug. 'We deal with it fine,' says Mendocino District Attorney Norm Vroman. 'It's the rest of the country that's all screwed up.'"

—From a 2001 *U. S. News* story

"The [Humboldt County] populace is more rural than urban, but even townsfolk are fond of gardening and buying local produce. Skills are multiple, allowing many people to make a living, and includes marijuana cultivation, which although pervasive is nevertheless only one economic activity."

—From "Sustainable Humboldt: Economic vision," by Jan Lundberg, originally written for *The Final Energy Crisis* (2004)

EROTIC UNIVERSITY
2260 15TH ST.
LOS ANGELES, CA
818-342-7566
WWW.EROTICUNIVERSITY.COM

Erotic University is a one-of-a-kind institution. At its campus at Entertanium Studios in downtown Los Angeles, the school offers a curriculum that includes classes like Swinging 101, Adult Toy Master Class, Adult Webmastering, and even the occasional course about religion and what the Bible says about sex and sexuality. And, yes, Entertanium specializes in porn production. What better setting for the Erotic University classroom—with its periodic table of sexual positions—than an adult film facility in the capital of the adult film industry?

STAR MAPS

HOLLYWOOD

I've made it; I've finally made it! After the brutal bus trip across the country—with some of the craziest, stinkiest people on the planet—I've finally made it to Hollywood! Welcome to paradise!

Wait a second. Those crazy, stinky people on the bus? They're just the tip of the iceberg. The Hollywood sign? Shrouded by smog. The Walk of Fame? I'm not even sure I'd want my star here.

Where's that bus? Can I get a ticket back home?

Seriously, though, Hollywood is a great place to visit, but don't look any strange person in the eyes. And lock your car. But no trip to Los Angeles would be complete without a stroll down Hollywood Boulevard past the very famous Grauman's Chinese Theatre and the who's who of weirdoes, from the guy with the sandwich board reading "CAST ME IN YOUR MOVIE!!!" to the gentleman with the aluminum foil antenna to Mars.

HUH?

INTEGRATRON
2477 BELFIELD BLVD.
LANDERS, CA
760-364-3126
WWW.INTEGRATRON.COM

The father of the Integratron, George Van Tassel, was a visionary scientist, a true UFO believer, and world-class nutball.

Located in the California desert so as to take advantage of a magnetic vortex emitted by Giant Rock—touted by proud locals as the world's largest freestanding boulder—the Integratron was designed by Van Tassel as a rejuvenation chamber and a time machine. Sadly, it doesn't function properly in either regard. On the plus side, its sonic acoustics are really funky—management holds that the wooden parabola known as "Integratron" delivers sound deep into cellular levels.

Guided tours are available for $5, but those in the know will opt for an $8 sound bath and soak for a half-hour in the resonance of nine quartz crystal singing bowls. The management touts the resulting "waves of peace, unbounded awareness, and relaxation of the mind and body."

Van Tassel didn't care much for the separation of church and science. He took architectural inspiration from the Bible, making the Integratron in the image of the tabernacles described in its pages. He also made much of the Integratron's geographic relationship with the Great Pyramids of Egypt. Like his plans to master time and death with the Integratron, both these correlations hold little water today.

WINCHESTER MYSTERY HOUSE
525 S. WINCHESTER BLVD.
SAN JOSE, CA
408-247-2101
WWW.WINCHESTERMYSTERYHOUSE.COM

In 1884, a soothsayer warned Sarah Winchester: "When you finish building your house, you will die."

Winchester took it to heart. Luckily, she was one of the Winchester Rifle Company Winchesters, so it was not a financial concern to hire guys to perpetually build stairways to nowhere and rooms too small for the smallest of people.

It follows that Sarah Winchester's house in San Jose was under construction from the day her fortune was told in 1884 to her death in 1922. The finished product, featuring 160 rooms, forty-seven fireplaces, 950 doors, and 10,000 windows, is now a tourist trap. I'm not sure if Winchester's spiritual advisor foresaw that development.

MUSEUM OF JURASSIC TECHNOLOGY
9341 VENICE BLVD.
CULVER CITY, CA
310-836-6131
WWW.MJT.ORG

Words don't do every museum justice. This is one of them. Exhibits delve into stink ants, fruit-stone carving, and human horns. Go see for yourself.

(Also see "Sasquest" for plenty more Huh? in California.)

GRUB

CALIFORNIA CUISINE

In the 1980s, something called "California Cuisine" blipped up on the national radar. It meant something that melded ethnic traditions into miniscule portions at premium prices. However, California's juggernaut-style population growth means California Cuisine is really, well, everything humans can possibly consume. California produces as much cheese as Wisconsin and more than half of the country's fruits, nuts, and vegetables—including all of the nation's commercially grown almonds, artichokes, dates, figs, kiwis, nectarines, olives, persimmons, pistachios, prunes, raisins, and walnuts.

So what is California Cuisine? The better question is, what isn't?

SLEEPS

YOSEMITE BUG
6979 Hwy. 140
Midpines, CA
209-966-6666
www.yosemitebug.com

I like the Yosemite Bug far more than I like Yosemite Valley, which isn't saying much because I don't like the overbuilt Valley much at all. Sure, it's beautiful and all, but I prefer my majestic natural beauty without the Disneyland-style crowds. But I really like the Yosemite Bug, one of the smartest, funkiest, and all-around best lodging establishments in the country.

The Bug is the antidote to the Valley twenty-five miles away in that it feels like everything perfectly fits. From the swimming hole to the web of walkways connecting the facilities, the Bug subtly perches on what basically amounts to a forested mountainside. This arrangement makes for an invigorating walk from the restaurant/gathering place/ lobby to the parking lot above, but it also makes for a development that's organic to the landscape.

The range of rooms and rates is pretty mind boggling, from $18 hostel bunks to relatively upscale themed rooms with private baths (including a psychedelic Austin Powers one) for $115 in the summer.

The Bug Café is an award winner and a local favorite. Its grub is as satisfying for the money as anything I've had in California (one example: a chili-rubbed chicken breast with side of buttered garbanzos and carrots for only $7), and the beer is cheap, too (pints of Bud are $1.75 but there's also Guinness, Stella Artois, and Anchor Steam on draught), amazing considering the lack of booze-peddling competition in these parts.

At the base of the hill, there's that swimming hole, fed by its own miniature waterfall, looking just like paradise on a hot summer day.

MADONNA INN
100 MADONNA RD.
SAN LUIS OBISPO, CA
800-543-9666
WWW.MADONNAINN.COM

The grand dame of kitschy hotels, San Luis Obispo's Madonna Inn offers guests an outlet to indulge their darkest fantasies, whether it's caveman-style sex, or gypsy-style sex, or pioneer-style sex, or just plain old sex in a really tacky room. Each of the 109 rooms here are unique and hard to forget, unless you drink yourself into a stupor. And, based on the wallpaper, that is not recommended.

MISC.

VENICE BEACH
Los Angeles, CA
WWW.VENICECHAMBER.NET

Still the heart of California weird, the commerce that defines surfer cool on Venice Beach hasn't changed much since its Dogtown heyday. Cheap huts sell cheap sunglasses ranging from knockoff to kitsch. Head shops offer bongs, pipes, papers, and even more esoteric devices for the burning and inhalation of marijuana. There are also plenty of purveyors of food and drink (tacos and burgers and beer) and T-shirts, preferably emblazoned with ironic witticisms, pop-culture references, psychedelic imagery, or some combination of the aforementioned.

A massive mural of onetime Venice resident Jim Morrison looms over Speedway near 18th Avenue. (The Doors once played at local clubs.) Besides the Lizard King, there are also two landmarks of oddball architecture near Main and Rose Streets, just a few blocks from Venice Beach proper: a pair of Frank Gehry buildings fronted by a three-story pair of binoculars by sculptor Claes Oldenburg; and the nearby Venice Renaissance, adorned by a large clown in a tutu. That's right: a large clown in a tutu. The perpetually moving statue, fittingly called *Ballerina Clown*, is the work of Jonathan Borofsky.

Most of the Venice Beach experience is about hanging out and enjoying the vibe, which is pretty easy to do here. After all, it's a beach. Wander the main drag. Suntan. Take a dip. Walk the beach. Smoke a joint. Rent a cruiser. Eat some tacos and drink some beer.

SASQUEST:

THE HUNT FOR BIGFOOT

500 MILES, 3 DAYS, 1 STATE

We drove around a bend and suddenly saw Bigfoot. He was standing on the side of U. S. Highway 101 near Garberville, California, working as a whore for the local souvenir industry.

This particular sighting was not of a living, breathing, eight-foot primate, but rather a hunk of wood carved into Sasquatch form by a chainsaw, perched on road's edge in front of Legend of Bigfoot, a souvenir stand hocking T-shirts, woodcarvings, toothpick holders, and a healthy section of Bigfoot paraphernalia.

I was with Dave, former rock-and-roll comrade in a semi-defunct band, biologist, and ER nurse at a city hospital in San Francisco. His background in biology makes him an excellent colleague for a Sasquatch search. His background in emergency medicine will also come in handy if Bigfoot happens to be a junkie or has a screwdriver stuck in an orifice. Hopefully, neither of these scenarios will come to pass.

We had just started a three-day expedition in prime Sasquatch country: Northern California's Humboldt, Trinity, and Del Norte Counties, including Redwood National and State Parks. Our plan included stops at several sites where Bigfoot had allegedly been spotted over the course of the past century, including Bluff Creek, where the famed Patterson film—of a Sasquatch walking and turning to look at the camera in stride—was shot in 1968.

Early on, Dave estimated the likelihood of Bigfoot's existence at a mere 3 percent. I was more optimistic, but ultimately a skeptic as well.

At Legend of Bigfoot, I bought a couple of books, one being the earnest *Field Guide to the Sasquatch*. They made a nice addition to the book already in my possession, *Bigfoot! The True Story of Apes in America*, by noted crypto-zoologist Loren Coleman. A cryptozoologist is a scientist specializing in animals yet to be formally discovered, like the Loch Ness Monster, chupacabra (a. k. a., the Puerto Rican goatsucker), and, of course, Bigfoot. Dave bought a "Bigfoot Country" ballcap.

I asked the cashier, a middle-aged woman from upstate New York, about Bigfoot. She didn't think it was real, concluding, "It's pretty hard· to believe in something when there's no evidence." She told me to look around the corner at a new Bigfoot woodcarving slated to replace the older one out front.

The new sculpture was kinder and gentler than the intimidating lame duck: man-sized and grinning widely, more reminiscent of a Disney character than a stinky backcountry ape. It was modeled after a $5,000 Bigfoot suit worn by employees in summers past but now worn-out, the cashier told me. I grabbed a brochure before I left; of course, the smiling, synthetic Bigfoot was front and center.

That night at the Lost Coast Brewery in Eureka, I asked the waitress about her knowledge of Bigfoot. She relayed a

18

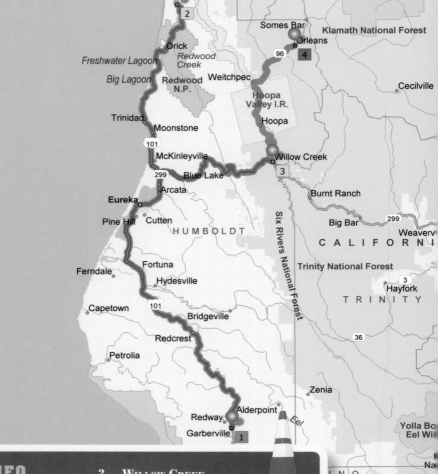

Marble Mountain Wilderness

Klamath

Klamath National Forest

Somes Bar

Orleans

4

96

Cecilville

Redwood Creek

Orick

Freshwater Lagoon

Big Lagoon

Redwood N.P.

Weitchpec

Hoopa Valley I.R.

Hoopa

Trinidad

Moonstone

McKinleyville

101

299

Blue Lake

Willow Creek

3

Arcata

Eureka

Burnt Ranch

Big Bar

299

Weaverv

Pine Hill

Cutten

HUMBOLDT

CALIFORNI

Trinity National Forest

TRINITY

Six Rivers National Forest

Ferndale

Fortuna

Hydesville

3

Hayfork

Capetown

101

Bridgeville

36

Redcrest

Petrolia

Zenia

Alderpoint

Eel

Yolla Bo
Eel Wil

Redway

Garberville

1

INO

Na

Castle

0 mi

Pacific Ocean

TRIP INFO

1. **LEGEND OF BIGFOOT**
   2500 U. S. HWY. 101
   GARBERVILLE, CA
   707-247-3332

2. **REDWOOD NATIONAL**
   AND STATE PARKS
   707-464-6101
   WWW.NPS.GOV/REDW

3. **WILLOW CREEK**
   CHINA FLAT MUSEUM
   CA HWY. 299
   WILLOW CREEK, CA
   530-629-2653

4. **E-NE-NUCK CAMPGROUND/SIX**
   RIVERS NATIONAL FOREST
   CA HWY. 96
   530-627-3291
   WWW.FS.FED.US/R5/SIXRIVERS

personal camping story: "I once heard something crashing around by my tent in the middle of the night."

"Maybe it was an elk?" I countered.

"It sounded two-legged, not four-legged," came her response. "But we didn't have a flashlight."

Dave leafed through the field guide and noted that August was peak Sasquatch sighting season. According to the chapter "A Sasquatch Profile," Bigfoot ranges from six to eleven feet in height and 700 to 2,500 pounds on the scale. He is lipless, with elongated arms, bangs drifting down his sloping forehead, and presumably omnivorous. His legendary footprint is typically around eighteen inches from tip to tip, but tops out at nearly two feet—i. e. size 22 or so.

We talked about what Bigfoot represented. "It seems like it's more about man than animals," said Dave. Bigfoot's nearly human footprint sealed his relationship with man, we decided, the wild man, bigger, hairier, and—most importantly—undetectable, not omnipresent.

After dinner, we set our sights on the campground at Gold Bluffs Beach near Orick, but every last site was already occupied. We headed to a hike-in campground, Flint Ridge, but didn't get to the trailhead until after sundown.

Dave studied at a sign across from the parking lot.

"Is that the trail?" I asked.

"I don't think so," answered Dave, who then located what turned out to be an exceedingly steep trail through thick greenery down to an empty beach—no Bigfoot and no campground. We drank beer and fell asleep in the sand behind a big rock. Sunrise was spectacular, but we were pretty sure we'd broken camping regulations.

After the brief but grueling hike back to the car in the morning, it turned out the sign Dave was reading the night before actually indicated the Flint Ridge Campground was a quarter-mile in the other direction. Whatever. No big deal.

Driving north to Crescent City, Dave got a glimpse of the scale of the Redwood forest. He adjusted his likelihood of Bigfoot to 5 percent.

No one in town had much to say about Bigfoot. A ranger at the HQ of Redwood National and State Parks more or less dismissed my line of Sasquatch questioning; her air of superiority slightly deflated our intentions. An hour later, Stephanie Jones, the owner of local eatery Circle J's, also said the legend was pure phooey, but gave us a bag of killer pasta salad and seven huge chocolate chip and walnut cookies to aid us in our search.

Later that day we drove twenty miles west (where it was about thirty degrees hotter) to Gasquet and spoke with Karenda Dean, a ranger with the Six Rivers National Forest. Like the clerk at Legend of Bigfoot, she didn't think the whole Sasquatch thing had much credibility, but she was not convinced either way.

"I believe ... whatever," she said. "This place is so absolutely rugged, I say, 'Why not?'" She also told us that Six Rivers was not the heart of Bigfoot country and pointed us in the right direction, down to Bluff Creek near Weitchpec. Dave and I immediately made plans to camp there the next night.

Dean also made mention that Bigfoot predated the white man and cryptozoology, that tribes such as the Huppa and Saskit had legends of big, wooly recluses. According to *Field Guide to the Sasquatch*, cultures in just about every corner of the world have cryptozoological counterparts, from the Himalayan Yeti to the Brazilian Mapinguary.

The Oh-mah-'ah, Kala'litabiqw, Steta'l, and Tsiatko are just a few of the big, hairy men who inhabit the mythology of the native tribes of the Pacific Northwest. Legend often holds that they splintered off a given tribe's family tree eons ago, forsaking culture for the forest, rarely to be seen again.

Coleman's *Bigfoot!* describes a sighting by a video crew in Jedediah Smith State Park, our next stop after chatting with Dean in Gasquet. The crew included a former Playboy Playmate and the Bigfoot in question was allegedly sporting an erection. Coleman covered the sexual nature of this and other sightings and notes that such reports do little to cultivate the authority of true believers.

While hiking in the vicinity of the so-called "Playmate Video," Dave suggested that Bigfoot sightings might just be the manifestation of a latent geek fantasy to be a solitary, ultra-masculine beast. We later saw a deteriorating stump that bore a slight resemblance to Bigfoot, and a couple of rocks, and agreed that the forest was so big and so thick that even an eight-foot-tall mammal might go undetected, especially if he had any brains whatsoever.

At the hike's turnaround point—about three miles into a dense forest populated by 200-foot redwoods and relatively oversized ferns—we stopped at a small waterfall and listened. A noise penetrated the warm inland air. It was heavy machinery at a construction site a few miles away, undoubtedly encroaching upon what once was prime Sasquatch habitat.

That night, we drove a good fifty miles south to Dry Lagoon—a picture-perfect coastal campground—set up camp, and watched the sunset from the beach. After polishing off the killer pasta salad earlier donated to our cause, we heard a rustling in the woods. Not the result of twenty-inch tootsies, the crunching turned out to be a lone

Homo sapiens blatantly violating the "No Wood Gathering!!!" rule posted on the bulletin board below.

We got a good jump on the next morning and hiked Fern Canyon and Friendship Ridge near Gold Bluffs Beach, through a primeval redwood forest kept especially cool and comfortable by the coastal breeze. We saw banana slugs and talked about naming our firstborn after Greek deities—Ares and Persephone emerged as possibilities. But we missed a sign on the trail, one that later showed itself to be as plain as day. This amounted to about an hour of clueless wandering in the woods.

"If we can't even see or read manmade signs, how do we expect to find Bigfoot?" I asked Dave.

Regardless, we still reached our next destination, the town of Willow Creek, by two o'clock that afternoon after a ninety-minute drive south and east, and grabbed lunch next door to the Willow Creek China Flat Museum—best known for its Bigfoot wing.

The people at the café had little to say about Bigfoot.

"I don't know," one woman said bluntly. "I really don't like talking about it."

Her much younger co-worker added two cents to the discussion. "I once saw a tall figure down on the river. I don't know what it was. It was dark."

After lunch, we braved the August heat and walked next door to the museum. The Bigfoot collection included newspaper articles, plaster casts of feet and hands and hips, photographs, and artwork (including a portrait influenced by Renoir or van Gogh and a diorama influenced by neither). A historical display informed us that the first newspaper report of Bigfoot was in nineteenth-century New York, over a century before tracks were allegedly discovered near Willow Creek in 1958. Of special note were two display cases dedicated to the impact of the Sasquatch on popular culture, with numerous children's books, toys, and a trio of Bigfoot-inspired board games.

All in all, the exhibit was a bit underwhelming, but the gift shop's selection of Sasquatch souvenirs actually topped that of Legend of Bigfoot, with three sizes of figurines, plus books, T-shirts, shot glasses, key chains, videos, and even "Bigfoot's favorite jelly"—blackberry.

A guest book invited the museum's visitors to memorialize their Bigfoot run-ins in words. Many were clearly from the prepubescent set, describing an encounter at camp or in the suburbs or elsewhere. One man's entry purported to have seen a Sasquatch on Mt. Shasta; another on the banks of Bluff Creek, where we planned to camp that night.

The volunteer at the museum's front desk, an overly enthusiastic middle-aged woman, was a hardcore believer. She seemed like she might have been involved with some sort of Sasquatch cult. Maybe she'd been brainwashed by a cryptozoologist or somebody.

"There was a sighting over the 4th of July up at Happy Camp," she said. "Talk to the guy at the deli."

"Have you seen one?" I asked.

"No. But I've heard a lot of stories. And I believe totally —there's no doubt about it." She told us about a number of credible sightings by well-known scientists. "The more you read the books about Bigfoot, the more you get a bigger idea that he exists," she said knowingly.

She went on to tell us, among other things, that the Russian Bigfoot snuck into barns in the middle of the night to braid the horses' manes, an undertaking that seemed more likely the work of an idiot savant hairdresser than Sasquatch's cousin.

A half-hour at the museum having satiated our curiosity, we visited a grocery store before driving thirty miles north on California State Highway 96 to the E-Ne-Nuck Campground. It was just a mile or so down from the best access from Highway 96 to Bluff Creek, on which Roger Patterson shot the famous Bigfoot film in 1968, albeit a good twenty miles from where we were.

After pitching a tent and resting in the shade, Dave and I headed into the dinky town of Weitchpec to see if we could get some wisdom from a native of the local Yurok Tribe. The only words we heard were, "Store's closed." So we drove back to the vicinity of E-Ne-Nuck and hiked down a precipitous bank to the confluence of Bluff Creek and the Trinity River.

The area was alive. There were tadpoles in the river and snails in the creek. Lizards scrambled on the rocks. There were also plenty of blackberries (Bigfoot's favorite!); Dave and I wiped out a couple of brambles.

With water from the creek, I crafted a big footprint on a rock with my hand. It evaporated in approximately one minute.

It was so rugged down at Bluff Creek that there was really no way to explore the vicinity on foot. We'd need horses or hovercraft or something like that. So Dave and I trudged back up to the car at dusk and made for E-Ne-Nuck for the night. We ate orzo-and-couscous burritos. (Dave, who manned the camp stove, is a vegetarian. I, like Bigfoot, am an omnivore.)

"I'm going to put on my neon shirt," Dave said after dinner.

"You're going to scare Bigfoot," I joked. I contemplated Bigfoot as Dave read a book about the night sky he'd purchased the morning before.

Several minutes passed. I had an idea: "We should come up with a fictional ending for this travelogue, just in case Bigfoot turns out to be a no-show." Dave kept on reading.

Just then, a local Yurok elder walked up to our campsite. He asked if we'd seen anything unusual and sniffed at the air. "Omah," he said.

"Excuse me?" said Dave.

"Omah. Oh-mah-'ah. The hairy one."

"Bigfoot?" I interjected.

The elder laughed. "The white man's name for Omah, yes. Do you know the truth?"

Dave and I told him that, sadly, we did not. He instructed us to sit down and lit a pipe.

"Many moons ago, the people—my people—living in what is now California and Oregon had a civil war and split into two groups. One group—those who became the Omah—resisted innovation, in terms of language, technology, and culture. The other group, from which I am a descendant, did not.

"Those who resisted change rid themselves of all of belongings—even clothing—and drifted deep into the forest. Both groups have for the most part co-existed peacefully ever since.

"Omah has a culture, a history, and a language, but they intentionally keep such things to the bare minimum. The prime cultural directive is not 'Make as much money as you can.' It is 'Stay away from man.'"

The smoke from the elder's pipe was clearly playing tricks with my head. His human form was shifting right before my eyes. Thick red hair sprouted from his head and worked its

way down his body, engulfing his flannel shirt and then his jeans. His frame expanded from 5'9" to 8'4". His voice deepened. I rubbed my eyes.

The elder was Bigfoot. He stood up, extending his nearly ten-foot frame, and told us—

Dave coughed, interrupting my faux ending to this story. By this point, he had lost interest in this fictional possibility; he was studying his book about constellations. Crickets chirped and logging trucks roared.

I suggested another alternate ending: "Bigfoot comes into the tent in the middle of the night and converts us to Scientology."

We laughed and drank Tecate and tequila and whiskey. "It's so hard to find

ourselves in the woods, let alone a stinky, hairy, 2,500-pound ape," I said.

Dave continued to study his constellation book in anticipation of a very starry night. "Cassiopeia, maybe," he said to himself.

I was taking notes on a legal pad. I struggled to remember my own quote. "What did I say?"

"It's so hard to find ourselves in the woods," responded Dave, "let alone a stinky, hairy, 2,500-pound ape."

EPILOGUE

In the middle of the night, Bigfoot didn't preach the gospel according to L. Ron Hubbard, but strange sounds did awake me sometime around two in the morning. I'm not sure what was behind them, but it was unlike anything I've ever heard. I was scared and shined my light but saw nothing. My ability to describe it to Dave the next morning was pitiful and quickly got worse. I'm not sure it was Bigfoot, but I'm willing to give the big guy a 15 percent chance of existence, nearly double than Dave's final opinion of 8 percent.

THE PACIFIC NORTHWEST

Pacific Northwesterners, sometimes called Cascadians, are so laid back that it's hard to tell if anyone actually works up here. Maybe it's the rain, but coffee breaks tend to dominate the mornings and naps fit right in with the gray afternoons. But when the sun does peek out from behind its cotton-like curtains, that's when nobody in Cascadia works at all.

Besides getting the bulk of the West's rain, Washington, Oregon, and Idaho also get quite a bit of radicals who fled Northern California but didn't quite have the guts—or, alternately, had too many outstanding arrest warrants—to cross the border to Canada. The region's high concentration of eccentrics hits a zenith in Portland, Seattle, and the Idaho wilderness.

Beyond the weirdoes, the Pacific Northwest's cast of characters includes loggers, sailors, environmentalists, and geeks. The latter flock to the area for its thriving high-tech industry, with Washington-based Microsoft leading the way. With that pesky anti-trust suit out of the way, Bill Gates and friends have thankfully gotten back to the task of making more money than they could possibly count, let alone spend.

All of the Northwest's extremes somehow harmoniously balance or cancel each other out in the end. The mellow vibe is counteracted by all of the strong coffee. A spectacular summer makes up for the rainy season. The loggers (who help cancel out the trees) and the environmentalists stare each other down. And all of the geeks nicely complement the weirdoes by making it clear that there are things worse than talking to an imaginary friend: You could be loudly jabbering tech jargon into a hands-free cell phone, boring everyone within earshot.

IDAHO (POP. 1,366,000)

- The deepest river gorge in the U. S. is Hells Canyon on the Idaho-Oregon border. At its deepest, it's more than 8,000 feet from rim to river.

- The Pacific Northwest is home to the world's largest sportswear company (Oregon's Nike), the worlds' largest software company (Washington's Microsoft), and the world's largest living thing (a 2,200-acre fungus growing in eastern Oregon).

OREGON (POP. 3,559,000)

- Oregon's state nut is the hazelnut. The state grows 99 percent of the country's hazelnut crop.

WASHINGTON (POP. 6,131,000)

- Washington is the only state named after a president. Previously, Minnesota and Mississippi had both considered the moniker, but ultimately rejected it.

BIG THINGS AND OTHER ROAD ART

FREMONT TROLL

UNDER THE AURORA AVE.
BRIDGE AT N. 35TH ST.
SEATTLE, WA

Like something out of a postmodern fairy tale, a gigantic concrete troll lurks under the Fremont Bridge, mangling a VW Beetle in its massive meathook.

My first encounter with the Fremont Troll found him deserted and alone, the highway traffic above providing a mechanized beat. I climbed the Troll's shoulder for a better look and noticed his eyes were made out of headlights. The columns supporting the overpass gave the area a Hall-of-the-Mountain-King aura, an industrial fantasyland. After a bit, a couple of carloads of noisy tourists cut the atmosphere a little bit, but could not overpower the rumpled majesty of the Troll.

FUNNY FARM

64990 DESCHUTES MARKET RD.
BEND, OR
541-389-6391
WWW.FUNFARM.COM

Founded by Gene Carsey and the late Mike Craven in 1977, the Funny Farm is a secondhand store that slowly morphed into a sculpture garden of the bizarre. It is one of the greatest roadside attractions in the Pacific Northwest. The place is definitely funny but not much of a farm— unless you count the bowling balls growing in the flower-bed (and the bowling ball seeds for sale in the gift shop). Well, that and the sixty or so llamas, goats, turkeys, and other barnyard familiars who call the place home. Among the purely funny things on the premises: a pink flamingo nesting area, a totem pole of tires, a dollhouse with a mini TV/kaleidoscope perpetually playing *The Wizard of Oz*,

Reading:

- *Still Life with Woodpecker*, Tom Robbins
- *Rains All the Time: A Connoisseur's History of Weather in the Pacific Northwest*, David Laskin
- **Anything by Chuck Palahniuk**

Viewing:

- *Napoleon Dynamite*
- *Kurt and Courtney*
- **Most anything by Gus Van Sant**

Listening:

- *Nevermind*, Nirvana
- **"Louie, Louie," the Kingsmen (recorded in Portland)**
- **Anything by Sleater-Kinney or Jimi Hendrix**

To-do Checklist:

- **Jig for squid in Puget Sound**
- **Get a tattoo**
- **Bring your black lab and a cup of coffee to the dog park**
- **Pack an umbrella**

"The Beaten Path" and the surrounding area that's off of it. And if you're in the market for a wedding, the heart-shaped Love Pond here might be just the spot—especially if you show up on the annual free wedding day.

HAT 'N' BOOTS
6400 S. CORSON AVE.
SEATTLE, WA
WWW.HATNBOOTS.ORG

In 1955, a Seattle entrepreneur saw the future of selling gas and it was a big cowboy hat and even bigger cowboy boots. Hat 'n' Boots was born along Highway 99. Elvis filled his car here in the 1963 dud *It Happened at the World's Fair*. The choice to build massive Western apparel as a means of selling gasoline looked prescient.

But I-5 came and stole much of the traffic from 99 and the lights went off once and for good at Hat 'n' Boots in 1988. Weeds took over the asphalt. Brave skateboarders occasionally scaled the hat and did ollies on the brim, but that was about it. By the late 1990s, the bulldozers were salivating.

But a number of Seattleites took up the cause of preserving the old mimetic landmark; one parade in 1997 involved protestors in cowboy duds. It worked, with one condition: Move it or lose it. So the Georgetown neighborhood offered space in the new Oxbow Park and both Hat 'n' Boots were peacefully relocated to their new home in 2003.

R. I. P.

JIMI HENDRIX, 1942–1970
GREENWOOD MEMORIAL PARK
350 NE MONROE ST.
RENTON, WA

When we first drove in to the cemetery, there were no obvious signs of a grave of a rock star. We noticed a few guys milling about a marker adorned with a few American flags, but a funeral was in progress nearby, so we parked and started walking the loop. I had a day-glo psychedelic shrine in mind, but didn't note anything to that effect. We saw a maintenance guy and asked, "Where is Jimi Hendrix's grave?"

It was the American-flagged stone after all, so we approached as the nearby service was ending. Next to grandmother Nora and the future sites of his parents was the unassuming stone where Hendrix is laid to rest. Under a nearby tree sat a couple of slightly haggard gentlemen. One approached, unshaven in a ballcap, and taped a piece of wax paper on the stone and proceeded to rub it with a crayon, making an impression. After a few minutes, he introduced himself as Rod and explained how he'd been camping out nearby and coming to Jimi's grave on a daily basis.

He let us create our own rubs with his wax paper and crayons; we gave him a few bucks each in return. Rod said he was looking to, "drink beer and smoke pot and howl at the moon." He said he'd met Eric Clapton here last week, and Steven Tyler earlier in the month. Tyler was apparently buying a plot for his own grave.

As I rubbed, Rod kept critiquing my technique: "Not that hard!" "Not so soft!" He eventually told his cohort

that I "made a hell of a rub." As we gave the guys our best on our way out, a guy in a homemade Jerry Garcia T-shirt, wielding a brown-bagged beer, appeared on a bike. So did a family. We shook Rod's hand and took off, wondering how much longer the authorities would allow him to loiter at Jimi's grave.

(I don't know if Rod is still hanging out there or not, so bring your own wax paper and crayons if you want to do a rub.)

BRUCE AND BRANDON LEE, 1940–1973 AND 1965–1993
LAKEVIEW CEMETERY
1554 15TH AVE. E
SEATTLE, WA

Near the center of Lakeview Cemetery are the resting sites of martial-arts movie legend Bruce Lee and his son Brandon. When I visited, a mix of Asian families and goateed slackers gathered about their ornate markers, posing for photos and leaving roses, photos, and coins behind. Bruce's grave has a yin-yang on it and an inscription detailing his importance to the martial-arts world before his untimely

death at the age of thirty-two in 1973. Conspiracy theorists say he was killed by a "touch of death" applied by a master martial artist angered by Lee giving away ancient secrets to the West.

His son Brandon, whose life was cut similarly short during the making of *The Crow* in 1993, is by his side, and also the subject of several conspiracy theories. Looking out over Lake Washington, I though to myself, fate was not very kind to the Lee family.

ERNEST HEMINGWAY, 1899–1961
KETCHUM CEMETERY
IDAHO HWY. 75
KETCHUM, ID

"Papa" Hemingway's brilliant, miserly economy of words and spare, matter-of-fact prose have long been guideposts. And his zeal for adventure and travel is hard to fathom: After driving a Red Cross ambulance in World War I Italy—and sustaining severe injuries from mortar and machine gun fire—Hemingway took to a life of roaming and writing, spending time in Paris, Spain, and Africa before settling for most of the 1940s and 1950s in Cuba, where he capped his career with *The Old Man and the Sea*, published in 1952.

After Fidel Castro's revolution prevailed in 1960, Hemingway relocated to Sun Valley. Illness and writer's block took hold, and Hemingway was increasingly stuck inside at home. Unable to roam or write, he took his own life a year later.

VICE

BOB'S JAVA JIVE
2102 S. TACOMA WAY
TACOMA, WA
253-475-9843

This coffeepot-shaped tavern in Tacoma, Washington, is a relic from a time when buildings were built to look like the business housed within. This is the only one left in these parts. The name of the place comes from chimpanzees, Java and Jive, that once called the place home. The chimps are

gone, replaced by the dirty punk rock bands that take the stage of this landmark joint with an extremely over-the-top jungle theme.

EASTLAKE ZOO TAVERN
2301 EASTLAKE AVE. E
SEATTLE, WA
206-329-3277
WWW.EASTLAKEZOO.COM

The name says it all—a menagerie of bikers, students, and other assorted rowdies howl and bark and shriek at the moon in this cavernous neighborhood pool hall. Established in 1974, the Zoo is owned cooperatively by the bartenders and serves a lot of beer and a little bit of wine. Take your pick of darts, pool, or pinball, or nursing cold Rainiers at the bar or on the well-worn balcony. Loud, ornery, and authentically Seattle.

STRIP CITY
PORTLAND, OR

Rip City might just be short for Strip City, which has the nation's highest concentration of all-nude strip clubs with

full-bar service. According to some solid investigative reporting by *Willamette Week*, Portland boasts 7.74 strip clubs per 100,000 residents, outpacing even Las Vegas (5.85).

Most places tend to have an either-or philosophy with full nudity and full bars; even Vegas (proper) has laws barring the doffing of g-strings where quaffing of alcohol is allowed. In Portland, this philosophy goes out the window, making Portland the natural destination for any bachelor party originating in Seattle.

What's most interesting is that this attitude stems from an article in the Oregon Constitution that affords free speech more protection than do the constitutions of almost every other state, bolstered by a series of Oregon Supreme Court Decisions in the 1980s. This translated to the state passing down a hands-off policy to local lawmakers regarding strip clubs and their ability to dispense alcohol: No regulations or zoning requirements has long been the statewide status quo.

STAR MAPS

EVEL KNIEVEL'S SNAKE RIVER CANYON DEBACLE

Knievel's earthen ramp is visible from the Buzz Langdon Visitor Center, overlooking Snake River Canyon, 858 N. Blue Lakes Blvd., Twin Falls, ID.

Robert "Evel" Knievel turned himself into an international superstar more through P. T. Barnum-style publicity than successful motorcycle jumps. Even the stunt that really pushed his star into the big time—jumping the fountains at Caesar's in Vegas—ended in a crash that broke Knievel's pelvis, femur, and both wrists, not to mention gave him a concussion that left him in a coma for almost a month. No wonder he became a superstar.

But the daredevil needed constant publicity to keep his celebrity machine optimally whirring. He saw an opportunity for a story when federal authorities barred him from jumping the Grand Canyon, so he looked north to Twin Falls, Idaho, and decided to give Snake River Canyon a try. He leased some private property on the canyon's edge, but his vehicle— the X-1 Skycycle, a two-wheeled gizmo that looked like the offspring of a motorcycle and a rocket ship—didn't quite fly the 1,580 necessary feet on September 8, 1974, to clear the canyon, no thanks to a parachute that deployed early. The Skycycle ended up on the canyon floor, half submerged in the Snake River. But at least Knievel didn't end up in a coma for a month. In fact, he escaped pretty much unscathed.

MATT GROENING'S PORTLAND
PORTLAND, OR

We just might have an entire generation of people who have spent more of their lifetimes watching *The Simpsons* than they did studying. Which means that in just about any bar in the country, you can spark up a conversation concerning the names of the "Seven Duffs" (for the record, that would be Tipsy, Queasy, Surly, Remorseful, Sleazy, Dizzy, and Edgy) or your favorite *Treehouse of Horrors* segment. Completists will certainly want to cruise Portland—the childhood home of *The Simpsons* creator Matt Groening—and drive on the numerous streets that inspired monikers on the show: Lovejoy (as in Reverend), Flanders (as in Ned), Quimby (as in Mayor), and even Terwilliger Boulevard (as in Sideshow Bob). Most important might be Evergreen Terrace, the street on which Groening grew up in Portland and the Simpsons stay the same age on in Springfield.

NAPOLEON DYNAMITE'S HOMETOWN
PRESTON, ID
WWW.PRESTONIDAHO.ORG

In 2005, the Idaho State Legislature passed a resolution commending Jared and Jerusha Hess for their "vision, talent, and creativity" in writing and producing *Napoleon Dynamite* on location in Preston, Idaho. The legislation, which goes on to cite Uncle Rico's football skills and Napoleon's love of tater tots as positive emblems of Idaho's culture, cites the movie as a key driver of increased tourism in the state. The Preston Chamber of Commerce jumped on the bandwagon and started a cottage industry by selling T-shirts with quotes from the movie, hats emblazoned with the slogan "Preston—Home of Napoleon Dynamite," and maps to the locations seen in the movie. In June 2005, the town threw its first annual Napoleon Dynamite Festival, with "sweet bike" races, look-a-like contests, and tetherball and tater-tot-eating competitions.

ARCHIE MCPHEE
2428 NW Market St.
Seattle, WA
206-297-0240
www.mcphee.com

This is bar none my favorite store to browse in the country, even if I have no intention of buying. Bin after bin of plastic animals, strange educational posters and recipe cards from the 1970s, Elvis impersonator playing cards, Jesus and Freud action figures, dogs playing poker on velvet—this is a surplus store of the strange and the tacky. I love it. One particularly cash-strapped holiday season, all of my family members received odd gifts purchased on a shoestring from Archie McPhee.

GRUB

VOODOO DOUGHNUT
22 SW 3RD AVE.
PORTLAND, OR
503-241-4704

With a menu that includes the Dirty Snowball, the Memphis Mafia, and the Triple Chocolate Penetration, Voodoo Doughnut is the brainchild of Tres Shannon and Kenneth Pogson. (The Nyquil glaze with Pepto-Bismol filling has been sadly discontinued due to regulatory issues.) Shannon and Pogson's dinky, art-laden doughnut shop does legal weddings under a velvet portrait of Isaac Hayes and showcases oddball musical acts and performance artists. The hours are ideal for drunks and insomniacs: 10 p.m. to 10 a.m., closed Saturday morning and Sundays.

COFFEE CULTURE

It is said that Seattle has more coffeeshops per capita than any other city in the country. Beyond the independents, java juggernaut Starbucks has its worldwide headquarters in the Emerald City. According to some estimates, nearly a quarter-million shots of espresso are drunk here daily.

Even coffee idolatry isn't beyond the norm here—Seattle's Coffee Messiah (1554 Olive Way) is just the place to worship the java idol every morning, maybe even chow on a vegan doughnut or a tasty gluten steak sandwich. Their slogan: "Caffeine Saves!"

SLEEPS

MCMENAMINS GRAND LODGE
3505 PACIFIC AVE.
FOREST GROVE, OR
503-992-9533
WWW.MCMENAMINS.COM

This historic Masonic lodge is now a great place to get away in Portland, even if you live there. Originally built in 1922, the lodge charitably housed elderly residents in its early existence. Then the McMenamins, kingpins of Portland's bar scene, made a deal with the Masons and renovated the place into a hotel, opening its doors in 2000.

The place boggles the mind. Artful and sprawling, the Grand Lodge has a microbrewery, a soaking pool, a Frisbee golf course, a theater showing cool flicks for the guests, an array of restaurants and bars. The bathrooms are shared and the rooms have cool murals on the walls, some covering the life and times of a former resident of the lodge, others dedicated to pop culture icons like Bob Dylan.

The McMenamins have done similar things with other properties in the Portland area: They converted a couple of schools into similar places to eat, drink, and sleep and have also remade historic hotels in their distinctive style.

ACE HOTEL
2423 1ST AVE.
SEATTLE, WA
206-448-4721
WWW.ACEHOTEL.COM

Seattle has always been about the future. The Space Needle has just been begging for science fiction to take the place of reality for more than forty years. Thankfully, the Ace Hotel isn't stuck in the past or even the present. The rooms are minimalism meets *Total Recall*, white and clean and sleek with bursts of artificial nature (i. e., huge photo murals of the great outdoors above your bed) and high technology. It's also surrounded by hip nightlife—including the legendary Crocodile Cafe three blocks away—so you don't have to stumble very far. The one and only thing that feels retro at the Ace? The rates, around $75 to $100 a night.

SYLVIA BEACH HOTEL
267 NW CLIFF ST.
NEWPORT, OR
541-265-5428
WWW.SYLVIABEACHHOTEL.COM

Few things go together like a lazy beach vacation and a good book—chips and salsa are the only pair I can think of that comes close. Continuing on the beach/book theme, the literary traveler can't expect to do any better than the Sylvia Beach Hotel, an old clapboard hostelry on a bluff above the beach. Rooms are divided into three categories—classics (high-end), bestsellers (mid-priced), and novels (budget), each named after a writer of renown. The classics include Mark Twain, with a complete library of his works; Dr. Seuss, with a big picture of the Cat in the Hat, is a bestseller; and Oscar Wilde is a more modest novel—I'm not sure he would agree. Rooms run around $90 to $130.

DOG BARK PARK INN B & B

U. S. Hwy 95
Cottonwood, ID
208-962-3647
WWW.DOGBARKPARKINN.COM

Sleeping with a dog can be comfy and cozy, but sleeping in a dog sounds kind of sick. Unless, of course, the dog in question is the World's Largest Beagle, which is exactly the case at Dog Bark Park. Guests enter three-story Sweet Willy near his belly and sleep in his chest or his head. The proprietors, who specialize in chainsaw carvings of posed canines, operate a gift shop on the premises and opened the inn in 2004. You can spend the night in Sweet Willy for about $88.

Fittingly, dogs are accepted.

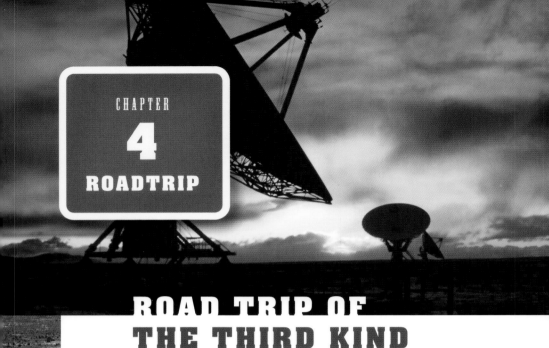

ROAD TRIP OF THE THIRD KIND

5 DAYS, 1,657 MILES, 4 STATES

In Roswell, alien cultures made contact. The whole incident seemed so random. A flash of red light across the way. It was random chance that we saw anything.

In Roswell, New Mexico, the two aforementioned cultures came together at Bud's, a package liquor store and lounge fronted by a bright neon sign on North Main Street. They were Caucasian cowboys and African-American players. The DJ veered from Jay-Z to Travis Tritt and nobody batted an eye. The scene wasn't without its occasional moments of friction, but ultimately the pursuit of the mass happiness usurped that of the individual. The numerous females present were relatively genre-agnostic, but the guys were exclusively pure country or hardcore hip-hop.

I clinked beers with Nygard, my half-Dutch, half-Norwegian cohort from college, and watched the somewhat surreal scene with bleary eyes. We had just finished the Atomic Vacation (see Chapter 6) and were now on the trail of intelligent extraterrestrial life, momentarily sidetracked by the terrestrial organisms at Bud's. We dropped by expecting very little except a nightcap at a deserted bar. An hour later, it was getting late, but the dance floor was a hypnotic sight. Two Latinas were doing that faux-spank dance—with each other.

The only hang-up between us, more beer and a later night, was a very long drive the next day. We were going to the Very Large Array in Socorro, New Mexico, and then trying to make it to my parents in Tucson by dinnertime. I'm getting soft. I left Nygard at Bud's after one beer. He ambled back to our room across the street at the Frontier Motel a short while later. The Frontier is one of those ideal roadside crash pads, clean and retro, with all the amenities (continental breakfast, pool, etc.), for all of $35 a night.

Earlier that day, we saw absolutely no evidence of any UFO crash on Boy Scout Mountain, roughly fifty miles west of Roswell in the Capitan Mountains. As legend has it, William Ragsdale had been camping here with his girlfriend on the night in question in July 1947. They witnessed a bright blob streaking across the sky and it crashed into the mountainside, killing the aliens inside.

We had arrived at the jeep trail to the Ragsdale site in the early afternoon and hiked for about two hours in search of space junk, UFO wreckage, skeletal remains of aliens, and fresh air. We only found the fresh air.

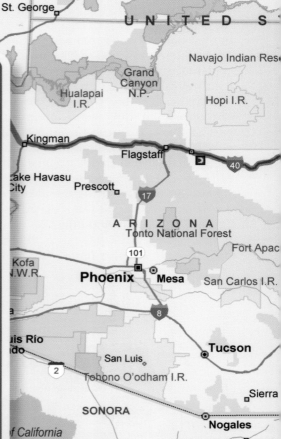

Round
Mountain

N E V A D A

Tonopah

Pioche

Nellis A.F.B. 6

Death
Valley
N.P.

TRIP INFO

1. **Bud's Lounge**
   3017 N. Main St.
   Roswell, NM
   505-622-9503

2. **Frontier Motel**
   3010 N. Main St.
   Roswell, NM
   800-678-1401
   WWW.FRONTIERMOTELROSWELL.COM

3. **Boy Scout Mountain**
   Lincoln National Forest
   Capitan, NM
   505-434-7200
   WWW.FS.FED.US/R3/LINCOLN

4. **International UFO Museum**
   and Research Center
   114 N. Main St.
   Roswell, NM
   505-625-9495
   WWW.IUFOMRC.COM

Uinta
National
Forest

Price

28

70

Richfield
U T A H

Cedar City

15

St. George

U N I T E D S

Navajo Indian Res

Grand
Canyon
N.P.

Hualapai
I.R.

Hopi I.R.

Kingman

Flagstaff

40

Lake Havasu
City

Prescott

17

A R I Z O N A
Tonto National Forest

Fort Apac

Kofa
N.W.R.

101

Phoenix   Mesa

San Carlos I.R.

8

...a

uis Río
...do

2

San Luis

Tucson

Tohono O'odham I.R.

Sierra

SONORA

Nogales

...of California

43

Cananea   M

5. **VERY LARGE ARRAY**
   U. S. 60, 50 MILES WEST
   SOCORRO, NM
   505-835-7000
   WWW.VLA.NRAO.EDU

6. **LITTLE A'LE'INN**
   NV HWY. 375
   RACHEL, NV
   775-729-2515
   WWW.LITTLEALEINN.COM

7. **AREA 51**
   CLASSIFIED, BUY A MAP AT THE
   LITTLE A'LE'INN

8. **UFO WATCHTOWER**
   2.5 MILES NORTH OF
   HOOPER, CO
   ON CO HWY. 17
   719-580-7901
   WWW.UFOWATCHTOWER.COM

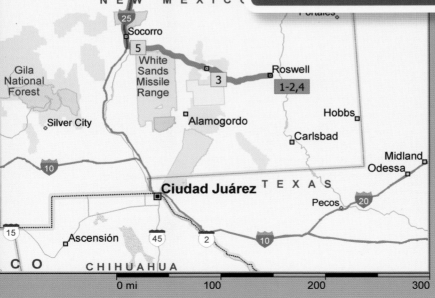

"So I guess this is a good time to ask if you think there is life on other planets," I said during the hike.

Sure, answered Nygard, citing Martin microbes.

"Intelligent life," I clarified.

"I don't know," he responded. "But I read somewhere that it is possible aliens could come to Earth and think humans were transportation systems developed by the dominant life form here—bacteria."

I had another theory. The Capitans, also known as the home of the real Smokey the Bear, were about halfway between the Trinity Site and Roswell. The infamous alleged UFO crashed here just two years after the planet's first atomic detonation in 1945. Atomic testing could well have attracted aliens two light years away, I speculated. If these beings had perfected the art of interstellar travel (well, nearly perfected—they crashed, after all), they certainly could also have come up with interstellar atomic-blast-detection technology.

Extrapolating on that hypothetical, the UFO that went down in '47 might just have been on a reconnaissance mission, just making sure our nuclear capabilities weren't a threat to a civilization in their particular solar system. The limited evidence of extraterrestrial life that's emerged in the time since could merely be a sign that Earth is akin to an anthill to their advanced alien perspective, and therefore not worthy of their time, diplomacy, or further exploration.

My intensive theorizing on Boy Scout Mountain dissipated sometime between dinner and the discovery of Bud's later that night. I'll blame it on the beer.

The next day the plan was to detour about 100 miles to the Very Large Array en route to my folks' place in Tucson, Arizona. (We skipped the International UFO Museum and Research Center because we'd both already been there on previous trips.) Nygard and I had developed the plan the day before, but I was having second thoughts. A bit hungover and road weary, I played the devil's advocate. "If we drive all the way to the Very Large Array (VLA), we probably won't make it to my parent's until after eight o'clock.

My mom's planning dinner. I'm not sure if we should go."

Nygard was adamant. "What? We should definitely go. I'd like to see it—it's going to be quite impressive."

"I've seen it. I saw *Contact.* I've seen pictures."

Nygard wouldn't accept that. I was won over after remembering Arizona didn't observe daylight savings time, meaning we would gain an hour once we left New Mexico.

Nygard, of course, was right. The VLA was one of the most impressive displays of high technology I'd ever seen. The size, scale, and scope of the twenty-seven radio telescopes—with eighty-foot dishes and 230 tons of girth—is striking, as is the fact that they move these things around on three thirteen-mile-long arms of railroad, spreading out to focus and coming together to zoom out for a look at the big picture. The big picture in question, of course, is deep outer space.

After scanning a few displays in the visitor center, Nygard and I embarked on a walking tour. The first stop demonstrated the power of the parabola. Two white dishes faced one another with about thirty feet in between. A tight spring of an antenna held a black rubber cork out a foot or two from each dish's center. Nygard approached one as I positioned myself in front of the other.

He spoke into the chunk of rubber affixed to his dish.

"Can you hear me?"

It sounded like he was sitting right next to me. Amazing.

"Yes, it sounds like you're right here. Can you hear me?"

Of course, it didn't take long for our discourse to hit rock bottom.

"What happens if you TALK REAL LOUD?" queried Nygard.

"Fuck!" I yelled back.

I screamed into the thing one more time for good measure. But point taken: Parabolic dishes have the awesome power to amplify waves of all kinds.

The walking tour snaked past various structures en route to the foot of one of the gargantuan radio telescopes.

As I retreated, the disc churned and chugged, and rotated a little bit, its sights adjusted to better peer at something in a galaxy far, far away.

While nobody listens for extraterrestrial communiqués on headphones like Jodie Foster in *Contact*, scientists have utilized the VLA to unlock some of the universe's most arcane secrets. While signs of intelligent life have been elusive, the discoveries made here run the gamut from other universes to supernovas to evidence of the Big Bang.

Our route took us to Tucson, Arizona, and Vegas for a couple of days, and then Nygard and I resumed our search for intelligent life in the universe 150 miles north of Sin City in Rachel, Nevada.

Located on Nevada Highway 375—a. k. a. "The Extraterrestrial Highway"—Rachel is best known for its primary business, the Little A'Le'Inn, the motel/souvenir shop/diner/bar that had a cameo or two on *The X-Files*. I asked about a room—doubles went for $40—but the extremely sleepy nature of Rachel (pop. 100) made us decide to get as close as we could to Area 51 and then drive into the night to Mesquite, Nevada, just a stone's throw from the Arizona border.

I bought a postcard and a 33-cent map to the boundary of Area 51 and left the Little A'Le'Inn in my rear-view mirror.

It was fifteen miles down gravel roads through a sparse forest of oddly formed Joshua trees surrounded by a bleakly beautiful mountainscape, eerie and otherworldly and the perfect gateway to Area 51.

The sun was setting, bathing the entire valley in golden light. It was blinding at times.

Then we were there. There was a "No Trespassing" sign and a line of orange pylons extending into the desert. A jeep was perched on a nearby hilltop. If you crossed the imaginary line, you'd be at best arrested and slapped with a $600 fine. At worst, the armed guard in the jeep would shoot you: As the sign noted, "Use of deadly force is authorized." We obeyed that directive, but ignored the posted photography ban—mainly because the Little A'Le'Inn's map advised us that it was not enforced.

I thought this might be the least popular tourist attraction—if you can actually call it that—I'd ever visited. Regardless, I'd highly recommend it, especially for those who can only take Vegas for twenty-four hours or so. Deserted and mysterious, Area 51 is the perfect antidote. Driving a dozen miles on dirt roads to a spot with no casino, no resort, no nothing—well, this is a destination that has more in common with Antarctica than it does with Las Vegas.

The significance of the spot is the utmost secrecy surrounding it. What we do know is that the military has covertly developed and tested numerous aircraft here. We also know that security is very tight, and that's about it. After a credible scientist named Bob Lazar said in a 1989 TV interview that he'd worked on an alien spacecraft in the Nevada desert, Area 51 became synonymous with the government cover-up of UFOs.

I'd recommend the drive to the boundary. It's scenic and a one-of-a-kind destination. After a few photos, however, your options are limited. I wondered what security would do if you pitched a tent and tried to stay the night. Nygard had other ideas.

"Do you think they'd do anything if I took a leak on that sign?" he asked.

I laughed. "What if you pissed over the line into Area 51?"

"That would be an interesting charge: unlawful urination on top-secret government property," replied Nygard, smiling.

After burgers at the Alamo Truck Stop on U. S. 93, we drove for the most part in silence, broken only by the sounds of a Miles Davis CD on minimal volume, and checked into the Virgin River Hotel and Casino around ten in the evening. The smoky casino bar held no allure, inhabited by the infirm and unkempt, so we called it a day and went to sleep.

The early night made for an early start the next day, which was critical. We had a 500-mile drive in front of us, through the Navajo Nation and Four Corners country, some of the most ruggedly beautiful land on the continent. Halfway through the day, road-weariness won out. I passed driving duties over to Nygard and dozed on and off until we made it to South Fork, Colorado, around eight and grabbed dinner at the Hungry Logger.

It had been a long day but it wasn't quite over. After dinner, I was going to make sure no one was crashing at my grandfather's cabin outside of South Fork, and then make the round trip to nearby Hooper, smack-dab in the middle of the San Luis Valley and home of the UFO Watchtower.

It took me a little while to find my grandpa's old cabin in the nearby hills, but sure enough we found it, empty and bearing a spare key. We left for Hooper straight away.

New Agers and conspiracy nuts alike regard the San Luis Valley as one of the most mysterious spots on the planet. With an average elevation of 7,600 feet surrounded by thorny mountain ranges with several 14,000-foot peaks, the 4,000-square-mile valley floor is flat as a pancake. It stretches from northern New Mexico into southern Colorado and has legend after legend carved into its history: devils and demons entering and exiting through inter-dimensional portals, Bigfoot-like hominids, and—most recently—surgically precise mutilations of horses and cattle suspected to be the work of extraterrestrials.

In fact, the San Luis Valley's downright weird reputation dates back several millennia. According to *The Mysterious Valley* by Christopher O'Brien, which I picked up the next day at the UFO Watchtower's gift shop (it was closed when we arrived later that night), "There are secrets, secrets hidden for thousands of years among the craggy spires of mountains." (O'Brien also felt it necessary to disclose that his book was "not a work of fiction. As you will see, in Colorado and New Mexico's San Luis Valley, reality can be stranger than any fiction.")

The livestock mutilations—also called unexplained animal deaths, or UADs—started in 1967, when a filly named

Snippy was found missing her flesh from her shoulders to her nostrils. By 1975, the area's numerous mutilations were the Associated Press of Colorado's "Story of the Year" and decried by state politicians as an egregious affront to the local cattle industry.

"In a typical 'classic' case," wrote O'Brien, "the cow was found dead and drained of blood with no signs of struggle. The sex organs were neatly removed and their rectums 'cored out.' Other missing parts included eyes, ears, tongues, portions of the lips or snouts, teeth, patches of skin, or the hearts." The era was also marked by sightings of both flying saucers and silent black helicopters.

We got to the UFO Watchtower after a little difficulty seeing the sign in the black of night. It was basic, made of welded pipes and sheet metal, and offered an incred-

ible view of the night sky. The Milky Way was crystal clear. So was the scale of Earth in terms of the great infinity. It's a speck of dust that's home to me and Nygard and 6 billion similarly relatively infinitesimal humans.

It was getting cold; we were 7,553 feet above sea level and it was early October. We stared at the sky, watching, waiting, drinking beer, and getting colder all the while.

The owner rumbled up in a pickup. "You guys just here to watch?" she asked, making sure we didn't want to grin and bear the near-freezing overnight low at a $10 campsite.

"Yeah, just thought we'd see what we could see," I said. "How many sightings have there been here?"

"Thirty-four since we opened five years ago. I've been lucky enough to see twenty of them. All but nine were seen at night."

She left us to our own devices and drove away.

A few minutes passed and I broke the silence. "In science fiction, aliens are always presented in one of two ways: Either they want to be our friends or they want to kill us. There's never any middle ground."

"They'd have to be from an incredibly advanced civilization if they made it here," Nygard noted. "I think they'd be very peaceful, very serene."

"Unless," I countered, "they were from an incredibly homogeneous, religious society with an unyielding faith in its own god. Then they might look at Earth and all of its different religions and try to convert us—or else."

Nygard agreed that a fundamentalist sect of extraterrestrials might cause the world a few problems, especially if they were the only species on their home planet. Then he saw a falling star. I missed it. Half a beer later, I saw one. Nygard missed it.

"It would be so easy to be facing the wrong way when a UFO flew by," I noted. "One person can't even see half the night sky at once."

I turned one way, Nygard turned the other, and we stared into the night sky. Regardless, the UFOs were no-shows. This is one of those rare stories about flying saucers that ends without a close encounter of any kind.

THE ROCKIES AND THE SOUTHWEST

The West as portrayed in mass media—the cowboys and the Indians, the open range, the untouched wilderness— never truly was. Instead, it's a blend of fact and fiction that was first whipped up by Buffalo Bill, reinterpreted by Hollywood, and perpetuated by plastic souvenirs, beer and cigarette ads, and singers from Nashville. The region is also known for its wilderness and nature, similarly exploited by the advertising industry to sell everything from politics to laxatives.

Today the Western genre is a self-fulfilling prophecy for the entire region: Urbanites yearning for wide, open spaces and fresh air come here and buy cowboy hats and snap shirts and become cowboys as best they can. Eastern kids come out to commune with nature in tie-dyed shirts. Billionaires buy ranches and raise cattle for fun, not profit. Most of all, people come here from all over "for a change." But in the end, it's not all that different from where they came from. They're searching for a myth.

ARIZONA (POP. 5,744,000)

- In July 2003, Phoenix had its highest low temperature in history—97.6 degrees Fahrenheit.

COLORADO (POP. 4,601,000)

- In Leadville, the country's highest incorporated city at 10,200 feet above sea level, approximately one-third of the planet's atmosphere is below you.

MONTANA (POP. 927,000)

- There is about one elk, two deer, two antelope, and six humans per square mile.

NEW MEXICO (POP. 1,903,000)

- In 1999, state legislators passed a bill making "Red or Green?"—chili, that is—the official state question.

OKLAHOMA (POP. 3,524,000)

- On the grounds of the state capitol in Oklahoma City, there is an operating oil well dubbed Capitol Site No. 1—a. k. a. Petunia No. 1 because a flowerbed occupied the spot that was originally drilled.

UTAH (POP. 2,389,000)

- With 170 rooms and walls six to nine feet thick, the Mormon Temple in Salt Lake City required forty years to build—and non-Mormons are not allowed to enter.

WYOMING (POP. 507,000)

- The last time Yellowstone went volcanic and blew its lid—about 640,000 years ago—the explosion moved about 2,500 times the rock and earth that Mount St. Helens did in 1980.

A significant percentage of nineteenth-century white settlers saw the Rockies and gave up. After dragging themselves across the thicket of the Great Plains at a rate of twenty miles a day, who could blame them? Those mountains must have looked like certain death. Conversely, the Mormons who blazed the trail before them chose the area because it looked like a good place to bunker down in the face of the impending doomsday.

But the real certainty of one's mortality isn't reaffirmed by just the jagged elevation of the mountains, but also by the heat of the deserts. There's a reason that Arizona didn't become a state until 1912: Willis Haviland Carrier didn't invent air-conditioning until 1902. Without A/C, modern Phoenix would be a gas station and an inbred clan of sunburned slackjaws.

Despite the march of technological "progress," in a lot of ways, the Rockies and the Southwest still look like certain death to outsiders. There are beastly bears, precipitous canyons, paralyzing storms, and all sorts of other ways to get to the hereafter here. This is why most Yellowstone tourists stick to the relative safety of the roads and the overlooks, venturing into the "wilderness" without changing one's routine or—have mercy—missing a shower.

BIG THINGS AND OTHER ROAD ART

SWETSVILLE ZOO
Just east of I-25, exit 265 (Harmony Rd.)
Timnath, CO

Bill Swets is a farmer by trade, an artist at heart, and a tinkerer above all. His eponymous city zoo is populated with spiders, dinosaurs, dragons, and all sorts of other critters made of junk: car parts, agricultural implements, discarded sheet metal, and the like.

Today the zoo is home to about 150 metal beasties, not to mention an old boat and a sporadically open tenant gallery. A life's work with farm machinery robbed Bill of his hearing, but

Reading:

- *Fear and Loathing in Las Vegas,* Hunter S. Thompson
- *The Monkey Wrench Gang,* Edward Abbey
- *At Close Range: Wyoming Stories,* Anne Proulx
- *The Unabomber's Manifesto,* Theodore Kaczynski

Viewing:

- *South Park*
- *Raising Arizona*
- *Little Big Man*
- *SLC Punk*

Listening:

- *The Rat Pack: Live in Las* Vegas, Sammy Davis, Jr., Dean Martin, and Frank Sinatra
- *John Denver's Greatest Hits,* John Denver
- *Rock of Ages: 30 Favorite Hymns,* Mormon Tabernacle Choir
- *Live at the Starlight,* Drag the River

To-do Checklist:

- Get altitude sickness
- Skim *The Book of Mormon*
- Lose everything/vomit/cheat on your spouse (choose one) in Vegas
- Go skiing, get knee surgery (in that order)
- Hole up in a cabin and complain about the government
- Eat chili until transcendence strikes

he reads lips pretty good, enough to tell you what you need to know about the Swetsville Zoo.

TOTEM POLE PARK
HWY. 28A, 4 MILES EAST
FOYIL, OK

From 1937 until his death, Ed Galloway woke up at five o'clock every morning and worked past sunset. When he was finished, he'd incorporated about thirty tons of cement, 100 tons of sand, and six tons of steel into his masterwork, dubbed "The World's Largest Concrete Totem Pole," not that the competition is very intense.

But Galloway's ninety-foot totem is a sight to behold, with 200 carved pictures and color to spare (it's maintained by a Lawrence, KS, arts group). Galloway's big totem is definitely his pièce de résistance, but there's no shortage of other colorful and interesting work here, including a number of smaller poles and Galloway's colorful residence, a. k. a. the Fiddle House.

R. I. P.

EDWARD ABBEY, 1927–1989
PARTS UNKNOWN, AZ

Best known for environmentalist rants like *Desert Solitaire* and *The Monkey Wrench Gang*, Abbey was the mad poet of the American desert, and now he's a part of it. The lingering question: What part exactly?

After Abbey died in 1989, he was buried—sans embalming or coffin—in a secret location in the Cabeza Prieta

Desert in southwestern Arizona. Only a few people know the precise spot, and they aren't talking.

HUNTER S. THOMPSON, 1937–2005
OWL FARM
WOODY CREEK RD.
WOODY CREEK, CO

Hunter S. Thompson was a crazed wizard of words, ramped up on all sorts of potions and pills and powders, spinning tales that inspired scads of drug-fueled expeditions to Vegas, Aspen, and everywhere else.

Few writers leave an entire genre as their legacy like Thompson did with gonzo journalism. Especially when espousing politics or fury, or, at his best, both, his grammatical alchemy—equal parts substance-propelled introspection, skewed reportage, and verbal pyrotechnics—will be worth reading as long as English is in circulation.

A 150-foot monument dubbed the "Gonzo Memorial Fist" was unveiled at a memorial in August 2005; the monument doubled as a cannon that blasted Thompson's ashes all over the property. The two-thumbed hand (holding an upturned mushroom) was financed through the sale of a special-edition beer and donations from the Hollywood elite.

But the best way to pay your respects to the good doctor is probably hoisting a Molson at Woody Creek Tavern (Upper River Rd. in Woody Creek, CO, 970-923-4585), his onetime local haunt.

BUFFALO BILL, 1846–1917
CEDAR MOUNTAIN
CODY, WY, OR
LOOKOUT MOUNTAIN
987-1/2 LOOKOUT MOUNTAIN RD.
GOLDEN, CO

William "Buffalo Bill" Cody was the architect of the popularized, mass-media view of the West, and his fingerprints are all over popular culture to this day. But he signed a bad contract late in his career, lost most of his fortune, and died in Denver in 1917.

That's where the intrigue starts. The *Denver Post* and the City of Denver allegedly bribed Cody's sister to keep his body in Colorado. But he died in January, with frost gripping Lookout Mountain, where Denver leaders wanted to bury him, based on what his sister said were his wishes. So the powers that be put "Buffalo Bill" on ice until the summer.

A few months later, an anonymous old cowboy died in Cody, Wyoming, where locals insisted Founding Father William Cody wanted to be buried, on Cedar Mountain outside of town. So a trio of interlopers trimmed the dead cowboy's beard and transported him down to Denver, where they proceeded to requisition the necessary key, swap bodies, and take the real deal back to the city that bore his name.

Cody's descendents are reputed to believe his final resting spot to be on Cedar Mountain in Wyoming, and not Lookout Mountain in Colorado, where the Colorado National Guard once guarded the grave in the 1940s (purportedly as a publicity stunt), well after the Mile High posse sealed the deal with several tons of concrete in 1927.

VICE

DENVER BEER

Per capita, Denver brews more beer than any other city. The losing candidate in the Colorado 2004 election for U.S. Senate was none other than beer scion Pete Coors, who needs no introduction. Better yet, Denver Mayor John Hickenlooper's claim to fame is the Wynkoop Brewery (1634 18th St., Denver, CO, 303-297-2700), the anchor of the Mile High City's nightlife-heavy LoDo—short for lower downtown—neighborhood. All in all, Denver has about 100 breweries and plays host to the Great American Beer Festival (www.beertown.org) every fall.

ST. PATRICK'S DAY IN BUTTE, MONTANA

Barnes turned to me and asked if I was ready for another.

"Get me a White Russian," I said.

The bartender said they didn't have any cream. We were at the M&M Club at about midnight. My dog Giblet was

with us, coincidentally leashed with six feet of green nylon. I believe I opted for a beer. Barnes and I are old high school pals, and we share a predisposition (genetic or otherwise) to go on the occasional bender. This was a good bender, celebrating St. Patrick's Day in Butte with tens of thousands of like-minded lushes for no good reason.

Barnes told me he was half-Irish and looked the part, with his fiery red hair and beard, and a glint of madness behind his prescription glasses. He'd been drinking Jamison-and-Cokes since about three in the afternoon, snapping six rolls of film between swallows. I'd been dabbling in White Russians and rum-and-Cokes, and we both had the occasional Budweiser (no green dye, thank you). I was taking sparse notes on the day's events in a weathered pocket pad. I'm barely Irish at all.

Butte, conversely, has a heavy Irish heritage, based on its roots as a mining town. Irish miners settled here in the 1860s and a lot of their kin remain in the region. Butte's St. Patrick's Day is an all-out party, with hordes of people milling about from dawn to well past dusk, boozing away in the crisp March weather. Everybody comes out—derelicts, politicians, tourists, and freaks. (Interestingly, all three banks in downtown Butte were closed on the St. Patrick's Day that Barnes and I attended, a Tuesday.) A parade kicks off the festivities in the morning but Barnes and I missed it. After that, people hold up their drinks and yell every couple of minutes. And people dance the jig. And people drink. And drink and drink and drink.

St. Patrick's Day gives way to St. Patrick's Night, where you don't have to look far for a fight. But if you're not looking, it isn't forced on you. I didn't see any drunken brawls with leprechauns standing on the bar, smashing bottles of bourbon over bald bikers' heads like a scene out of some B-movie, just a little pushing and shoving. One image stands out: A guy in those loose, zebra-striped pants with an elastic waist and ankles that were popular in the '80s, apparently prowling for a fight. Later, I saw him talking to a couple of cops in what looked like a post-melee questioning.

SIP-N-DIP
7TH ST. AND 1ST AVE. S
(IN THE O'HAIRE MOTOR INN)
GREAT FALLS, MT
406-454-2141

Great Falls might have lost the "falls" from its name to hydroelectric projects on the Missouri, but at least it's still got the Sip-N-Dip, one of the most distinctive bars in the West. First of all, it's a legitimate tiki bar, plastered with stuff collected by its pilot founder from all over the South Seas. Secondly, it's got great live entertainment in the form of Piano Pat, a fixture here since the 1960s. And most unbelievably of all, it's got a bank of windows behind the bar that offer a view into an adjacent pool. Mermaids swim during peak weekend hours, and a few oblivious couples have treated the entire bar to X-rated public displays of affections.

MEET RACK
210 W. DRACHMAN ST.
TUCSON, AZ
520-798-1235

Meet Rack proprietor Jim Anderson —a.k.a. God—has a deal for you: He'll brand you with a silver-dollar-sized portrait of his own bald-headed mug and in return you get 50 cents off your drinks at the Meet Rack ... for life. Jim also maintains scrapbooks containing photos of the more than 1,000 consenting customers he's branded.

But scarring one's skin for a booze discount is just the tip of the iceberg here. Using a condom machine in the women's bathroom activates an ear-splitting alarm that alerts the bar to the buyer's lustful intentions. There's a side room filled with antique sex gadgets, including an authentic chastity belt. Bras dangle from the ceiling and the walls are plastered in photos of Jim with patrons, photos of Jim with celebrities, photos of Jim by himself, and photos of a variety of scenes you've just got to see them for yourself. (As he said as he gave me the grand tour, "Here's Abe Vigoda, here's a dog fucking a pig, here's Jack Elam.")

There's also a small chunk of wall bearing Alcoholics Anonymous tokens redeemed for free drinks. Jim pointed to a nametag from a rehab facility and told me, "This guy's family spent $80,000 getting him sober. Within fifty minutes here, I had him drunk, branded, and sold him two T-shirts."

As the giveaway keychain bearing the image of "God's" profile brand reads, "I'll ruin your life."

CASSIE'S
214 YELLOWSTONE AVE.
CODY, WY
307-527-5500

The last brothel standing in a hardcore cowboy town until local lawmen cracked down on Cody, Wyoming's flesh-peddling industry in the 1950s, Cassie's is now one of the most hardcore cowboy bars on the planet. The heavily decorated walls here include numerous classic murals, a *Star* article about Tanya Tucker getting in a catfight on the premises (true, says proprietor Steve Singer), many stuffed animals and similar beasts' skinless noggins, and beer signs of all descriptions. Be prepared for one of the most innovative and lascivious country-and-western dance floors around.

(And don't miss the two great bars described in "Sin and Salvation"—the Double Down in Las Vegas and the Shooting Star Saloon in Huntsville, UT.)

VEGAS FOR CHEAPSKATES

The combination of extreme heat, massive hotel/casinos, and omnipresent neon tends to give visitors the green light to throw caution to the wind. Responsible people gamble away the mortgage, social drinkers black out, non-smokers choke down a couple of free packs. Then there's the re-creations of the New York skyline and the Eiffel Tower, the magic shows, and the hookers.

Personally, as cool as winning money sounds, I can't stomach the concept of losing money. My cheapskate strategy: keno. While your cohorts piss away their savings at the blackjack table, you're safe and sound in an easy chair, betting a buck or two every 10 minutes, and getting primo service when it comes to the free drinks—in the typically empty keno parlors, everybody sticks out like a sore thumb.

(Note: Despite the ad campaign, not everything that happens in Vegas stays there. For example, the clap and tattoos on your face will go home with you.)

NEVADA BROTHELS

The thirty legal brothels operating in Nevada are the only place you can buy sex in the United States without breaking the law. Legal in any county in Nevada with less than 400,000 inhabitants, the brothels pay the counties quarterly business fees, but the transactions are not taxed. Around a $50-million industry, legal prostitution in Nevada certainly pales to the illegal variety going on in Vegas, where the yellow pages are fattened by thousands of listings for escorts and adult entertainers.

COLFAX AVENUE

One of the longest urban streets in the country, Denver's Colfax Avenue has it all: adult bookstores, pawnshops, hookers, crack dealers, a gold-domed state capitol, sleazy

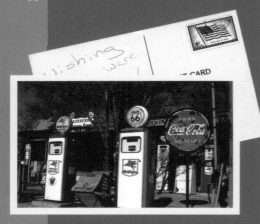

Trivia Box:

- Legendary daredevil Evel Knievel is from Butte, Montana.

- Joe Cocker resides in Crawford, Colorado.

- Estes Park, Colorado, filled in for Aspen in the movie *Dumb and Dumber*.

- Mork and Mindy lived at 1619 Pine St. in Boulder, Colorado.

- Brad Pitt was born in Shawnee, Oklahoma.

- The Sundance Film Festival brings the Hollywood elite, their entourages, and the paparazzi to Park City, Utah, every January.

- Jackson Hole, Wyoming, doubled as the Italian Stallion's Siberian training grounds in *Rocky IV*.

bathhouses, the largest restaurant in the Western Hemisphere, a U.S. Mint, shady bars, and plenty more. From tip to tip, Denver's Colfax Avenue is twenty-seven miles of blacktop with one foot in the plains and the other in the Rocky Mountain foothills.

Check out the landmark dive Lion's Lair (2022 E. Colfax Ave., Denver, CO, 303-320-9200), and grab late-night eats at Pete's Kitchen (1962 E. Colfax Ave., Denver, CO, 303-321-3139), where a breakfast burrito smothered in green chili shows up before you can finish a ciga-

rette. There are hookers east of Colorado Boulevard, drug dealers in Civic Center Park, and eccentrics just about everywhere. For a dollop of synthetic cheese, try Casa Bonita (see "Grub," later in this chapter).

STAR MAPS

LIBERACE MUSEUM
1775 E. Tropicana Ave.
Las Vegas, NV
702-798-5595
www.liberace.org

Love him or hate him, you've got to appreciate how far Liberace was willing to push the envelope into the realm of absolutely absurd excess. And this is just the place to see how far he pushed it. Check out his costumes. He had 400 of them. A lot of them set Libby back six figures—ask the docent to point out the one that was $750,000. Then there's the world's largest rhinestone, about the size of your head, forever rotating in a display case; rhinestone-clad cars and pianos; and other examples of celebrity kitsch at its most extreme form.

HUH?

OBSESSIONS, ER, CASTLES OF THE ROCKIES AND SOUTHWEST: MYSTERY CASTLE AND BISHOP CASTLE

MYSTERY CASTLE
200 E. MINERAL RD.
PHOENIX, AZ
602-268-1581

BISHOP CASTLE
CO HWY. 165
BEULAH, CO
719-485-3040
WWW.BISHOPCASTLE.ORG

Having contracted tuberculosis, Boyce Luther Gulley left his wife and daughter behind around 1930 and relocated to Phoenix for what he thought would be the short, tortuous end to his life. He started building a castle out of desert rocks and salvaged materials of all kind, and built it according to his daughter Mary Lou's whimsy, and lived a lot longer than expected. No city codes. No neighbors. Like that, Mystery Castle just kept getting bigger and stranger until Boyce died in 1945.

Bishop Castle is still a work-in-progress. Jim Bishop

started his big, strange castle in 1969 and now dubs it "the largest one-man construction project in the world." No kidding. With rocks collected in the surrounding forest, the castle has a 160-foot tower and is watched over by a steel dragon with a flamethrower in its throat.

COLORADO ALLIGATOR FARM
CO 17
MOSCA, CO
719-378-2612
WWW.COLORADOGATORS.COM

The Young family had been in the fish business, raising their trademark Rocky Mountain Tilapia for restaurants and local markets, for a decade when they struck upon an innovative way to get rid of the dead fish that would invariably float in their farm's waters. They bought 100 gators from Florida in 1987 and tossed them in geothermally heated

waters that simmered at a steady 87 degrees Fahrenheit.

The Youngs didn't know if the gators would survive the first Rocky Mountain winter, but pretty much all of them did, and as of the twenty-first century years, the Youngs are in the gator farm business, an unlikely enterprise in Colorado's San Luis Valley, the biggest (and probably the oddest) alpine valley on the planet. The farm is now home to about 400 gators (the Youngs got the breeding down pat after a few years), the largest of which are more than ten feet long and about 500 pounds. In the snow-packed winters, the big reptilians even like to climb up on the snow and soak in the sun's rays.

HAVRE BENEATH THE STREETS
TICKET OFFICE AT 3RD ST.
HAVRE, MT
406-265-8888

Downtown Havre (pronounced "have-her," as in, "You can have her") burned to a crisp in 1904. The buildings were gone but the basements survived, so merchants, lawyers, barmen, laundrymen, and even ladies of the night turned underground Havre into what might well have been the world's first enclosed shopping mall. A one-hour tour gives you a look at this odd first, complete with mannequins of Chinese laundry workers and prostitutes.

(Also see "Road Trip of the Third Kind" for plenty more Huh? in the Rockies and Southwest.)

GRUB

ROCKY MOUNTAIN OYSTERS
PROUD CUT
1227 SHERIDAN AVE.
CODY, WY

BUCKHORN EXCHANGE
1000 OSAGE ST.
DENVER, CO

TESTICLE FESTIVAL
CLINTON, MT
WWW. TESTYFESTY.COM

Oysters are hard to trust in the isolated Rockies, with their propensity to go bad fast and cause serious distress when they do. It follows that some coast-born migrant must have seen a bull's testicles and decided that they'd do in a pinch.

While the practice of eating wild kingdom genitalia goes back to ancient Rome, Rocky Mountain oysters have their origins in the West of the 1800s, when economical cowpokes tossed them on a hot stove and waited for them to explode like popcorn.

CASA BONITA
6715 W. COLFAX AVE.
LAKEWOOD, CO
303-232-5115
WWW.CASABONITADENVER.COM

Said to be the largest restaurant in the Western Hemisphere and without a doubt one of the tackiest, Casa Bonita opened in the '70s as a flagship for a chain that stretched from Little Rock to suburban Denver, the Mile High City's Casa Bonita is 52,000 square feet of sensory overload, centered on a two-story faux cliff with a pool underneath where costumed high-schoolers perform skits, inevitably ending with several if not all of the characters soaking wet. There are also fake caves, a mariachi band, a bizarre monkey mascot, an arcade, and little flags you raise when you want more food, which isn't held in high regard. I sneak salsa and tequila in when I go, which helps a little.

SLEEPS

KELLOFF'S BEST WESTERN MOVIE MANOR
2830 W. U. S. 160
MONTE VISTA, CO
800-771-9468
WWW.BESTWESTERN.COM

The only combination drive-in movie theater/motel I know of is located in Monte Vista, and would be the town's claim to fame except for the fact that there is a major stopover for Sandhill Cranes in the vicinity. The drive-in dates from 1955; the motel came about a decade later. Speakers in the rooms synch roughly to the movie shown on the screen in the motel's courtyard area. The windows are positioned for a view of the big screen, but alas they also have curtains, which my mom yanked shut here when she felt Cheech and Chong were intruding on our family vacation.

SHADY DELL RV PARK
1 OLD DOUGLAS RD.
BISBEE, AZ
520-432-3567
WWW.THESHADYDELL.COM

Motels and hotels can be time machines that take guests back to simpler eras. Such as the era before private bathrooms. Or the era before carpet cleaning. Or even those innocent pre-air-conditioning times. But RV parks are typically things of the present—at least until gas hits $5 a gallon that is—and Shady Dell is like none of the above: It's a retro RV park that does retro proud. It opened in 1927 and now rents vintage aluminum trailers with the works. Book a vintage 1947 Airporter now tricked out as a Tiki Bus or a dinky homemade trailer made in accordance with plans published in a 1952 *Popular Mechanics*. Or you can just get a regular old spot for your soon-to-be-obsolete RV.

MISC.

GREAT STUPA OF DHARMAKAYA
WHICH LIBERATES UPON SEEING
4921 COUNTY RD. 68-C
RED FEATHER LAKES, CO
888-788-7221
WWW.SHAMBHALAMOUNTAIN.ORG

As the eleventh reincarnation in a line of Tibetan Buddhist masters, Chogyam Trungpa Rinpoche was one of the prime catalysts behind the Tibetan Buddhism boom in the U. S. during the 1970s. He was also something of a drunken lech.

Trungpa's skull is entombed for eternity inside of a massive Buddha statue that sits lotus-style in a massive *stupa*—a towering spire serving as a monument to a great Buddhist teacher like old Chogyam himself. As a matter of fact, Trungpa, who died at the age of forty-seven in 1987 with a bum liver, is still so beloved to this day that the stupa his followers built is the largest in the Western Hemisphere: The Great Stupa of Dharmakaya which Liberates Upon Seeing (heretofore referred to in this text as T.G.S.O.D.W.L.U.S.) is 108 feet tall and one of the most ornate and durable structures you'll find in the middle of nowhere anywhere.

Built over the course of thirteen years at the Shambhala Mountain Center (with additional panels continually in progress), T.G.S.O.D.W.L.U.S may or may not liberate your consciousness at first sight, but it will almost certainly impress. Laden with multihued panels crafted by the most patient and skilled of craftsman, the stupa was built to stand for 1,000

years. It follows that the folks who engineered it specialize in nuclear facilities, utilizing concrete and miles of rebar.

Now T.G.S.O.D.W.L.U.S. is the visual centerpiece of the center, which offers a year-round curriculum focusing on meditation, yoga, and the teachings of Trungpa. Tent-cabins, hiking trails, and a meditation center round out the campus. Buddhists and non-Buddhists alike are welcome to visit or bunk down for the night.

RAMBLE ROAD TRIP HALL OF FAME

TRUMAN EVERTS:

FIRST PERSON TO GET LOST

IN YELLOWSTONE

There is something to be said for getting lost, provided you are found, and found alive. The progression from venturing to the known to scrambling in the unknown and back again covers a wide spectrum of human emotion, from the self-involved fuzz of daydreams to the frantic pulse of fear to the endpoint of elation once the term "lost" no longer applies.

If there were a hall of fame for getting lost, Truman Everts would surely be an inductee in its inaugural class. An accountant from Vermont, Everts holds the distinction of being the first person to get lost in what is now Yellowstone National Park, where getting lost is a snap. (I personally get lost almost every time I visit.) Not only was he the first person to truly get lost here, but he also was one of the most accomplished disorienteers in Yellowstone history. His lost expedition lasted thirty-seven days and included burns from sleeping on thermal vents, constipation from subsisting primarily on barely edible thistles, and a reward for his rescue, which was never paid out.

After getting separated from the Washburn Expedition in September 1870, Everts proceeded to lose his horse and most of his supplies and ignore all previously agreed upon rendezvous plans. Instead, he wandered aimlessly for more than five weeks until a mountain man/soldier of fortune named Jack Baronett took aim at what he thought was a bear waddling down a slope. Baronett put the gun down only after he realized the figure was not a grizzly but a very dirty Truman Everts crawling on all fours.

Everts' friends wouldn't pay the reward because Everts was still alive and plenty capable of rewarding Baronett himself. But the ungrateful accountant wouldn't pay up because he claimed he would have made it out on his own without any help. He went on to live another thirty-one years and even impregnate his twenty-something wife when he was in his mid-seventies. Clearly, his sperm had a better sense of direction than he did.

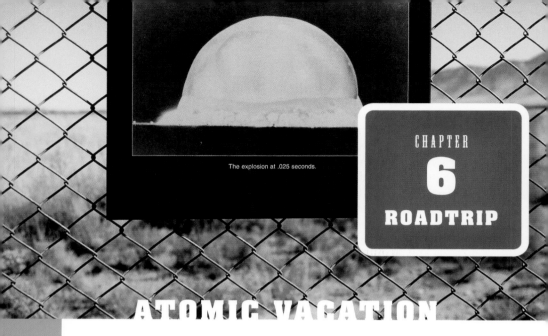
The explosion at .025 seconds.

ATOMIC VACATION

4 DAYS, 1,110 MILES, 3 STATES

The barbwire-topped fence next to the playground appeared to surround nothing, just a couple of slabs of concrete and a few odd vents and pipes sprouting from the ground. "No Trespassing," read a sign mounted on it. "Guard Dog On Duty," warned another.

Nygard and I walked along the fence-line and came to an open gate on a driveway to a tidy mobile home. The guard dog ambled into sight. A recently shorn sheepdog of some kind. It wagged its tail.

Beyond the guard dog and the mobile home, there was a guy rummaging through his car. There was also some lawn furniture. Despite the fence, the views of the surrounding farmland were quite nice and offered a peaceful rural atmosphere.

"Pete?"

The rummaging guy did not immediately respond. The sheepdog ran a playful lazy lap and sniffed at our heels.

"Pete?" I repeated.

Pete stood up and I made an introduction: "I'm Eric Peterson, the travel writer. This is my college friend Thomas from Amsterdam."

Pete was Pete Ambrose, employed by Weld County, Colorado. The easygoing guard dog, she was Casey. Pete and Casey and Pete's wife live above an Atlas E missile site just outside of Greeley, Colorado. The facility once housed a nuclear missile and a crew waiting for the order to annihilate the enemy if it came right down to it.

Working twenty-four-hour shifts, the crew here patiently waited for World War III from 1960 to 1965, until technological innovation shut Atlas Es down in favor of Atlas Fs, Titans, and Minutemen, superior methods of delivering an unearthly bomb the literal equal of a mountain of dynamite.

In the 1970s, the federal government handed the place over to Weld County, who turned it into Missile Site Park, hence the playground. The county also put in some campsites with a nice view of the Rocky Mountains on the horizon. Pete gives visitors tours of the facility by appointment and unlocks the place for county employees who want to get at the decades of files stored in the site's bowels.

After we followed him underground, Pete showed us the empty clamp that once held a nuclear missile and a display of atomic preparedness memorabilia: sleeves of antique crackers (emergency rations), how-to instructions for building fallout shelters, wax-sheathed medical equipment, drums of drinking water, and the like. I was particularly interested in an illustration of a happy family

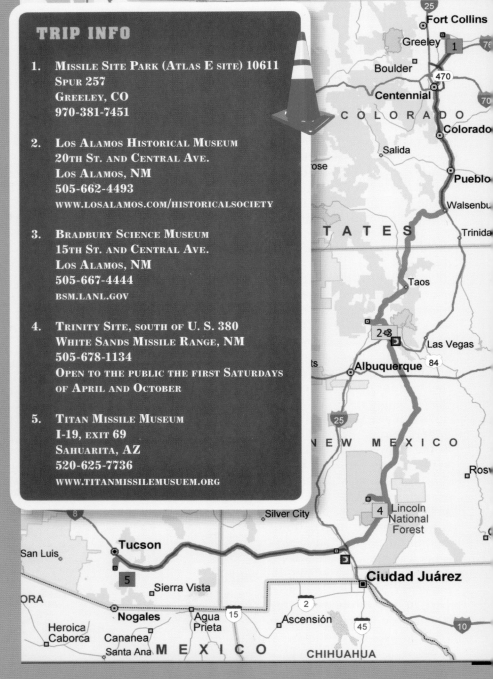

TRIP INFO

1. **MISSILE SITE PARK (ATLAS E SITE) 10611**
   SPUR 257
   GREELEY, CO
   970-381-7451

2. **LOS ALAMOS HISTORICAL MUSEUM**
   20TH ST. AND CENTRAL AVE.
   LOS ALAMOS, NM
   505-662-4493
   WWW.LOSALAMOS.COM/HISTORICALSOCIETY

3. **BRADBURY SCIENCE MUSEUM**
   15TH ST. AND CENTRAL AVE.
   LOS ALAMOS, NM
   505-667-4444
   BSM.LANL.GOV

4. **TRINITY SITE, SOUTH OF U. S. 380**
   WHITE SANDS MISSILE RANGE, NM
   505-678-1134
   OPEN TO THE PUBLIC THE FIRST SATURDAYS
   OF APRIL AND OCTOBER

5. **TITAN MISSILE MUSEUM**
   I-19, EXIT 69
   SAHUARITA, AZ
   520-625-7736
   WWW.TITANMISSILEMUSEUM.ORG

in an eight-by-eight fallout shelter, with little Susie tying her pigtails and smiling while Dad enjoys a relaxing smoke.

Pete pointed out a picture of civilians in Washington State inspecting an ICBM in the parking lot of a shopping mall. It looked like a popular roadside attraction with a military presence.

"Our society wasn't a closed society like Russian society was," he said. "In Russia, if you saw a truck with a missile and said something, they'd take you out and throw you in the gulag or something."

The bomb they dropped on Hiroshima was "a very poorly made bomb," Pete noted. "Only about 1 percent of it went off. But it killed 70,000 people initially and about 20,000 or 30,000 people died later.

"They've improved on it. This one here had a mushroom cloud seventeen miles high, structural damage ninety miles out, second degree burns thirty miles out. Anything within a two- or three-mile radius would not be there anymore."

"How strong was this?" Thomas asked.

"This was a four-megaton," Pete responded—the equivalent of 4 million tons of dynamite. "The Russians made a fifty-five-megaton bomb." Unfathomable.

Then he led us down a tunnel to the former control room where the crew waited for the launch command that never came. Now the area serves as a warehouse for county records. Posted on the wall was a story from the *Rocky Mountain News* about a Kansas couple who lived in a decommissioned Atlas E site.

"I read a book written after World War I," said Pete. "The author wrote that this was the most horrendous, horrifying thing that happened to mankind. I mean, they lost over 20,000 French soldiers in one day. The author thought there was nothing that could ever surpass this—anything. Then what did we have? World War II."

On our way out, I noticed a dead snake on the asphalt. Casey sniffed it with extreme caution.

Pete told us life at the site was "nice and quiet." He gave us a pair of Atlas E T-shirts, barking a warning to Nygard about the brownies in Amsterdam, and we were off.

We drove the hour back to my place in Denver. The Greeley trip was a warm-up for the meat of the Atomic Vacation: a visit to Los Alamos, New Mexico, where scientists developed the world's first atomic bombs in 1945, and the Trinity Site, 150 miles southeast, ground zero where said scientists set off the world's first manmade atomic explosion. The test at Trinity validated that these gadgets would indeed do serious damage to Hiroshima and Nagasaki and almost certainly force Japan to surrender, thus ending World War II.

After dinner, we watched the 1983 Matthew Broderick flick *WarGames*, which Nygard, a half-Dutch native of Norway, had somehow missed. I first saw it at a Colorado Springs mall when I was ten and the threat of nuclear annihilation was akin to national wallpaper, especially in the city that was the home of NORAD, one of the film's primary settings.

Despite several classic lines and performances—namely

Barry Corbin as General Beringer delivering dandies like "I'd piss on a sparkplug if I thought it'd do any good"—the movie felt pretty dated. The Internet, the War on Terror, and countless other post-Cold War developments had irrevocably re-shaped some of the themes it probed. But Nygard gave the flick a thumb's up nonetheless.

We got a seven-in-the-morning start the next day to Los Alamos (Spanish for "The Cottonwoods"), about a six-hour drive from Denver. Everything went smoothly and around lunchtime we rolled into town, which was built on a series of slender volcanic fingers separated by sheer cliffs and canyons.

Now 18,000 people strong, modern Los Alamos evolved out of the Manhattan Project, the codename for the development of the atomic bomb. From 1943 to 1946, 7,000 people lived in this top-secret city—scientists, soldiers, their wives and kids, and support crew. In the 1960s, government property was transferred to private ownership and the presence of the Los Alamos National Laboratory today makes for the most Ph.D.s per capita in the country.

Looking for lunch, the receptionist at the visitor center directed us to a doughnut shop that also sold chili and Frito pie. Both Nygard and I had the Frito pie.

Next, we went over to the Los Alamos Historical Museum. On the way, we noticed that the entire town was gathering on Central Avenue for the annual Homecoming Parade. While the Los Alamos High Hilltoppers were clearly the city's prime source of athletic pride, the all-American parade offered absolutely no clues to the town's origins as an atomic research site; the green hairspray shellacking several students' noggins seemed to be a hint of radioactivity until I realized that green and yellow were the school colors.

But time was of the essence; we abandoned the sidewalk for the museum. Hedy Dunn, the museum's director, gave us a tour and some insight into the city that arose from the scientific/military installation that came up with the world's first atomic bomb.

Dunn described the area's volcanic prehistory and quiet modern history as the site of an exclusive, expensive boarding school for toughening frail boys from back East, the Los Alamos Ranch School. The soft scions of the upper class (including renowned writer Gore Vidal for a semester) came to Los Alamos from 1917 to 1943, the year the U. S. Army wrote the headmaster a letter saying they were buying the property, like it or not. Then everything changed.

The Army gathered many of the world's most renowned scientists to help Manhattan Project leader J. Robert Oppenheimer in the task of developing an atomic bomb before Hitler or the Japanese did the same thing.

Dunn shared a number of interesting historical tidbits. Los Alamos originally had no name: Mail came to P. O. Box 1663, which also was listed as the birthplace on the birth certificates of those babies delivered in the city during the Manhattan Project. Because each Los Alaman had a special driver's license that offered them a degree of immunity from the law, local cops could do nothing to stop them from speeding into Santa Fe.

"Mail was censored both coming into the Project and leaving it," said Dunn. "One of the things that was censored was the fact that mail was censored. To get in, everybody had to show a pass, and even the kids had passes." She pointed out a picture of a Los Alamos resident's car during the Manhattan Project, emphasizing its nondescript license plate. "There's no state and no city and no year and no nothing."

This was perhaps the best-kept secret in human history.

Next on the agenda was the Bradbury Science Museum, a slick facility down the street that further illuminated the science and history of the atomic bomb and other discoveries made at the Los Alamos National Laboratory. It also had a couple of exhibits with a sociopolitical perspective: an anti-nuke display by the Los Alamos Museum Project (independent of the lab and museum) and a pro-nuke one by the similarly independent but otherwise opposite Los Alamos Education Group. Next to them was a comment book that hooked me more than the scientific exhibits. Unfortunately, the museum was on the verge of closing.

In the gift shop, I perused the atomic-related wares: books, DVDs (including *Dr. Strangelove* and *The Day After*), and even a handmade replica of the monument at the Trinity Site for $100—way too steep for my blood. I settled on a book, *Echoes of Trinity Site* by Jim Clayton, featuring text gleaned from the comments left in the book next to the pro- and anti-nuke displays at the museum.

That night at a motel in Socorro, I leafed through my souvenir. The "Point and Counterpoint" chapter has an entry from the Bradbury comment book that caught my eye: *"And a pessimist and a cynic wrote:* What can one say? Will mankind solve our problems—I think not!! *To which an optimist responded:* Yes, mankind can solve its problems. It always has."

Other comments in *Echoes of Trinity Site* struck me as profound: One ended, "The problem is war, not the means of waging it." "Thanks for inviting us—we don't have to go to school," a school kid wrote. Another was translated from Japanese: "I don't want to let the same thing happen twice. I'm from Hiroshima." I put the book down and turned off the light.

After a shower on Saturday morning, I pulled on the Atlas-E T-shirt Pete had given me in Greeley. Still sprawled out in the room's second queen bed, Nygard asked, "You want to wear matching shirts?"

The mental image of us wearing identical outfits at the Trinity Site made me laugh. Nygard elected to wear a white Liechtenstein T-shirt instead.

The Trinity Site saw its first public visitors in 1953 and the powers that be started hosting regular visitor days

once a year in the 1960s. Since the 1980s, Trinity has been open to the public twice a year: the first Saturdays in April and October. Typically, 2,000 to 3,000 visitors make it to ground zero.

We stopped at the Owl Café and Bar in San Antonio, New Mexico, about thirty miles northwest of the Trinity Site, for eggs and bacon. Decorated with pictures and statues of its namesake and some signed dollar bills sloppily stapled to the wall, the Owl was celebrating its sixtieth birthday with a few banners. It opened in 1945, the same year the open land to the southeast played host to the planet's first atomic explosion. The waitress said that Manhattan Project scientists indeed ate here, but offered little else in the way of information.

A half-hour later, we drove through the security gate leading into the White Sands Missile Range, where more than 40,000 rockets, missiles, and other projectiles have blown up since it opened in 1942. But by far the most significant explosion ever here took place at 5:29:45 a.m. on July 16, 1945. The chain reaction that started on the atomic scale almost instantaneously snowballed into 1,000-miles-per-hour winds and a shockwave that shattered windows 100 miles away.

We drove twenty miles south through surprisingly green desert. The traffic was neither thin nor thick. There were signs for deer crossing, followed by ones warning of some other exotic-looking horned animal crossing.

"I wonder if there's a crater," said Nygard.

"I have no idea," I responded. "I'm very curious what kind of crazy, otherworldly landscape we're about to see."

The parking lot bore a resemblance to any other tourist destination: plenty of families, RVers, and cameras hanging from necks. Atomic vacationing turned out to be far more popular than I thought.

Once within the fence-line, I found the Trinity Site remarkably nondescript. No crater, no glassy surface, no atom-carved canyonlands—the footsteps of visitors seemed to have a more pronounced effect on the dusty, grassy, high-desert plains than any cataclysmic event from sixty years ago. Even the radiation levels were said to be within the range of normal.

Many visitors spent their time scanning the ground and bending over to pick up rocks. They were looking for Trinitite—the green, glassy substance created when atomic energy seared the New Mexico sand. It's illegal to collect the stuff, and visitors were told this by security, posted signs, and the list of regulations every vehicle received upon entry. But none of this stopped people from looking.

After an hour or so of taking photos of the monument to the test and slowly strolling around the site, we'd felt we'd been there and done that. On our way out, we saw a sign reading, "Trinitite for Sale." We followed its directions to a rock shop about fifteen miles east of the turnoff to the Trinity Site.

Inside, Nygard inspected the Trinitite display case. He could not resist the lure of a $20 sliver as a souvenir. The rock shop's proprietor said a local miner legitimately collected his stock before the Atomic Energy Commission scraped the site in 1952.

"Today must be a big day for Trinitite sales," I said. "How much have you sold?"

The rock-seller paused, then asked, "Are you with the IRS?"

"No."

"Well, yesterday we did real well. Yesterday made our month."

Trinitite's $30-a-gram pricing of it made me think of other commodities.

"You should grind it up and snort it," I suggested to Nygard while driving away from the rock shop. "Or free-base it."

"I don't think anybody's ever tried that," said Nygard. The tone of his voice confirmed that he would not be the first.

According to the literature included with Nygard's gram, this stuff is as safe as milk. You could wear it on your neck without worry. Earrings, not a problem apparently. But could you eat the stuff?

"I'm not going to eat it," said Nygard. He was also confident that Dutch customs would have no problem with the extremely rare, lightly radioactive green pebble.

The next and final stop on the trip was the Titan Missile Museum, just south of Tucson, Arizona, where my parents graciously offered us room and board (and beer) free of charge. We took full advantage of their hospitality.

The next day we drove south on I-19 to Sahuarita, adjacent to the retirement mecca of Green Valley, and made our way to the museum. Of fifty-four Titan II sites in business from 1964 until President Reagan decommissioned them in the 1980s, this is the only one that was preserved in its natural state as a historic artifact. Most of the multi-million-dollar facilities were simply dynamited so the silos imploded, rendering them useless, although a fitness center took over the property above one former Titan II site in the Tucson vicinity.

We paid our admission and perused the displays on atomic and Cold War history before being ushered into a room for a short introductory video before a tour of the actual silo. The video's host was a middle-aged guy with a long ponytail—more hippie than would be expected—and his delivery was cheerful but a bit synthetic.

Then we donned hardhats for the main event: the tour of the silo and the command center, down fifty-five steps and through a myriad of blast doors and tunnels.

A missile combat crew of four people working in twenty-four-hour "alerts" staffed the facility when it was operational, the guide explained. When the new crew arrived each morning, passing through the nuke-resistant blast doors required four phone calls and the destruction of a slip of paper bearing that day's entry code. (They were supposed to burn it, but in the event of an ignition problem, eating it would suffice.) Then the old team opened the doors and let them in, soon sealing them in for their twenty-four-hour watch over the two keyholes that, if turned within five seconds of each other, would launch a missile bearing a nine-megaton nuclear warhead, 4,500 times more powerful than the bomb dropped on Hiroshima.

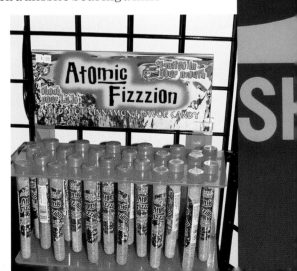

Most of the waiting that was done here at the Titan II site took place in the command center, a good-sized room with plenty of panels adorned with lights, switches, and buttons. Our guide pointed out the two aforementioned keyholes that would initiate the launch sequence. He described the heavily coded layers of theoretically foolproof security that worked the launch command down from the president to the team in the silo.

A real launch command would end with two men receiving one key each. As the keyholes were positioned so no one person could activate them by themselves, the guide asked for a volunteer. Nygard jumped at the opportunity.

Moments later, the guide and Nygard simultaneously turned their keys for five seconds. A moment passed, then a panel came alive with lights and a speaker warbled an obnoxious alarm. This is what nuclear war would look like to the members of the crew on duty.

In such an event, the four-person team would be stuck underground after they launched their missile waiting for additional orders, explained the guide. If these additional orders never came, it meant the aboveground world was devastated, the crew's superiors likely annihilated. But the site's emergency food and water supply would last thirty days, the same amount of time the oxygen re-circulator would provide fresh breathing air.

"That left the crew with a decision," noted the tour guide. "They could either wait thirty days and climb fifty-five steps to go out the blast doors and die of radiation poisoning, or they could wait down here thirty days and stay down here and die of oxygen deprivation."

"There's another option," I said to Nygard. "One of the them could have resorted to cannibalism to extend his own air and food supplies." We agreed this would be a fitting aftermath to something as gruesome and incomprehensibly violent as nuclear war.

After a peek through glass at the actual decommissioned Titan II missile (sans warhead, of course) as it was during the Cold War, the tour ended and we thanked the guide. Browsing the gift shop in the visitor center, I considered a Titan Missile Museum shot glass, a glossy photo of a mushroom cloud, and a missile-shaped pen, then settled on a $2.50 pamphlet called *Survival Under Atomic Attack*, a reprint of "The Official U. S. Government Booklet" distributed in 1950. Among the gems of advice contained within: "Don't rush outside right after a nuclear bombing," "Beyond a half-mile, your chances of surviving increase rapidly," and "Be careful not to track radioactive materials into the house."

Souvenir in hand, all that remained was signing the guest book. I scribbled my name, my hometown, and the comment, "I'm glad World War III didn't happen." Then I put the pen down and walked outside into the warm Arizona air.

TEXAS

With religious extremism, plenty of sun-scorched wasteland with oil underneath, and a conservative culture that strikes many as backwards, Texas is a lot like the Middle East. Only don't let a Texan hear you say that.

With the possible exception of Utah, Texas is the state most likely to secede from the U. S. into independent nationhood. Don't ask a Texan if they're part of the South, the Midwest, or the Southwest—this is Texas, goddamnit, big enough and tough enough to take on any state or region if it comes right down to it. And if Texas bordered Massachusetts or Vermont, it just might. But it borders Oklahoma and Arkansas, so things run pretty smoothly.

Texas is the land of Dubya, with the presidential ranch in Crawford and the boyhood home in Midland. Yup, the president is a Texan through and through—except, of course, for his Connecticut birthplace, his blue-blooded pedigree, and his C+-Ivy-League education.

Texas is also known for its diversity, ranging from West Texas, bleak and depopulated, to Hill Country, with rolling greenery and a hint of progressivism, to the East Texas of

TEXAS (POP. 22,490,000)

- Everything, and I mean everything (well, almost), is bigger in Texas: Forty-one of Texas' 254 counties are larger than Rhode Island. The 1,250-mile Texas-Mexico border is bigger than the rest of the U. S.-Mexico border. The Dallas-Fort Worth airport is bigger than Manhattan, and has the world's largest parking lot. The Texas State Capitol in Austin is the largest state capitol in the country. With 903 miles in Texas, U. S. Highway 83 is the longest highway in any one state. Texas has more than sixty trees that are the largest of their species in the country. Texas is also the largest petroleum-producing state in the U. S.

- Alas, you can't have it all. Texas is merely the second-largest state in terms of both population and size, trailing only California and Alaska, respectively. Detroit was ranked the country's fattest city in 2004—Houston a close second. And the U. S. Capitol is bigger than the Texas State Capitol. Dang.

- The nine-banded armadillo is the official Texas state small mammal. The funny little diggers' reflex to jump in the air when frightened—thus, the roadkill—is tempered by the fact that they give birth to identical quadruplets every time.

- Texas also has an official flying mammal (the Mexican free-tailed bat) and large mammal (the Texas longhorn).

- Caddo Lake in northeast Texas was the only natural lake in the entire state, until an oil strike in the area led to its damming in the early twentieth century.

Dallas, a city that seems to aspire to be Paris (France, that is), if only Paris weren't so damned French.

All this schizophrenia and machismo make for a bit of a volatile combo, but nothing that can't be pacified with a rack of ribs and a cold six-pack. Even Texans have their soft spots.

BIG THINGS AND OTHER ROAD ART

CADILLAC RANCH
I-40, EXIT 60 OR 62
AMARILLO, TX

Oddly enough, ten spray-painted Cadillacs on the side of the road are the American Dynasty's equivalent of Egypt's Great Pyramid at Cheops. At least that's the intent. Cadillac Ranch's automotive ingredients are buried up to their mid-section at fifty-two degrees, the very same angle as the slope of its inspiration-sake pyramids across the planet.

A San Francisco art collective known as the Ant Farm initially installed Cadillac Ranch in 1974 under the financial and creative auspices of helium heir Stanley Marsh 3. (Yes, 3 not III. He favors the Arabic numeral over the Roman standard. You get the picture? He's not the traditional type.) The cars were moved eastward in 1997 to escape Amarillo's encroaching sprawl.

Reading:

- *Friday Night Lights*, H. G. Bissinger
- Anything by Molly Ivins
- Anything by Larry McMurtry

Viewing:

- *Texas Chainsaw Massacre*
- *Dallas*
- *Lone Star*
- *Slacker* and *Dazed and Confused*

Listening:

- Anything by Stevie Ray Vaughan and Buddy Holly
- Most anything by the Butthole Surfers, Lyle Lovett, and Waylon Jennings

To-do Checklist:

- Eat your weight in beef
- Remember the Alamo—for your own safety, remember it like John Wayne did
- Learn to drawl
- Slack in Austin

Marsh's other public objets d'art include a pair of disembodied legs and donating a couple hundred civic-mimicking signs with odd slogans to the community. Now people's yard art include signs with all sorts of madcap slogans like, "Mime Assassin" and "Strong Drink Here" and two "No Two Signs Are Exactly Alike" signs, side by side.

ORANGE SHOW CENTER FOR VISIONARY ART
2402 Munger St.
Houston, TX
713-926-6368
www.orangeshow.org

Orange Show mastermind Jefferson Davis McKissack has been quoted as saying, "You could take 100,000 architects and 100,000 engineers and all of them together couldn't conceive of a show like this." The late Houston postal worker's show is dedicated to the healthful effects of the orange, thus *Orange Show.* More aptly described as a ramshackle,

Rube Goldberg-esque folk-art labyrinth clad in spinning wheels, concrete lions, and signs like "Clown found happiness by drinking fresh cold orange juice every day" and "I love oranges."

The big annual event at the Orange Show is May's ArtCar Parade. The momentary center for the international art car phenomenon draws around a quarter-million people and cars that look like bugs and rats, cars from the future, and cars covered with fruit and mirrors and all sorts of other weird shit. If you can't make it for the big event, there's a permanent collection at the ArtCar Museum (140 Heights Blvd., Houston, TX, 713-861-5526, www.artcarmuseum.com). The "Garage Mahal" focuses on art cars and other disciplines well outside of the mainstream art world.

CHINATI FOUNDATION
U. S. 67
MARFA, TX
32-729-4362
WWW.CHINATI.ORG

Fed up with the stifling Manhattan art scene, Donald Judd picked up stakes in 1972 and relocated to the absolute middle of nowhere: Marfa, Texas (pop. 2,500, give or take). He bought a few city blocks downtown and ended up taking the reins of the Chinati Foundation, a local arts organization, in 1985.

Judd installed some of his own work, and also invited a few longtime buddies from the minimalist community to take part. The results are mind boggling. The foundation's galleries are spread among the buildings at a former Army post and a building in downtown Marfa, with Judd's massive concrete blocks out front, Dan Flavin's neon installations occupying no less than three former barracks structures, and John Chamberlain's crushed-car sculptures in the downtown gallery.

This has all culminated in Marfa being buzzed about in New York and L. A. as the next Taos, and cracked adobes that sold for $30,000 in 2000 are selling for five times that in 2005. But nothing will ever change the fact that Marfa is a remote Texas town that's only sixty-one miles north of the Mexican border. It's a bit slow for New Yorkers in the long run, unless they're cut from the same bullheaded cloth as Judd.

R. I. P.

OLD RIP, 1890s–1933
EASTLAND COUNTY COURTHOUSE
100 W. MAIN ST.
EASTLAND, TX

Enthusiastic but cruel, the founders of Eastland, Texas, entombed a horned toad in the cornerstone of the Eastland County Courthouse when construction began in 1897. A new courthouse replaced it in 1928, and the cornerstone was cracked open in the process of demolition. To everybody's surprise, Old Rip (as in Van Winkle) was alive—or that's the story that became legend, to be later adapted into cartoons and tall tales and publicity stunts. Of course, the lizard died less than a year later. In 1997, Governor Dubya said Old Rip had "true Texas grit" on the 100th anniversary of his entombment. Old Rip's body is on display in a miniature coffin in the Eastland County Courthouse.

BUDDY HOLLY, 1936–1959
LUBBOCK CEMETERY
2011 31ST ST.
LUBBOCK, TX

In the early days of rock and roll, Buddy Holly proved that

geeks could rock as hard as anybody else. While the music industry has long focused on looks over sound, Holly had his trademark horn-rimmed glassed and the looks of an accountant. But he could play the hell out of his guitar and write killer songs—two skills Elvis notoriously lacked.

By the time the plane he chartered went down in a snowy Iowa cornfield, Holly was a certifiable rock icon ... and he was only twenty-two years old. The only thing of Holly's recovered from the crash site were his trademark spectacles, now on display at the Buddy Holly Center in Lubbock. Besides his marker in Lubbock Cemetery, another place to pay tribute is the bigger-than-life statue perched across town on Avenue Q between 7th and 8th Streets.

VICE

BORDER TOWNS

Beyond Hill Country and the Panhandle, there's another distinct region in Texas: the border zone. About 60 percent of the U. S.-Mexico border is fronted by Texas on the Rio Grande, making it one of the most culturally integrated melting pots anywhere. (El Paso-Ciudad Juárez is the largest metro area on any border on the planet.)

The border towns are transient places: Mexicans looking to get into the U. S. for jobs see them as way stations; Americans looking to eat, drink, or shop like them for the low prices and anything-goes attitudes. There's a lot of fun to be had down here—everything from the notoriously sleazy strip clubs to bullfights to very lax drugstores—but even more trouble to get into if you're looking for it.

Two of my favorite bars on the continent are in Mexican towns along the Texas border: the Corona Club in Ciudad Acuña (across from Del Rio) and the Kentucky Club in Ciudad Juárez. The Corona Club (Hidalgo #200, www.thecoronaclub. com) is owned by the Corona family of Corona cerveza fame, and was featured prominently in the movie *Desperado*—Cheech Marin was the ornery bartender. In reality, the place is not nearly as grim as it was in the movie—especially the bathroom—but still has oodles of character (taxidermy and cool photos line the walls) and even has a massive courtyard out back that serves as the best music venue in the region, north or south of the border.

With a swanky-but-weathered atmosphere that feels more 1950s than 2000s, the Kentucky Club (#629 Avenida

Trivia Box:

- Pay your respects to an oversized statue of Stevie Ray Vaughan in the Texas blues wizard hometown of Austin. Dudded up like Clint Eastwood in *The Good, the Bad, and the Ugly*, Stevie's just west of the First Avenue Bridge on the shores of Town Lake.

- John Wayne shot his jingoistic *The Alamo* not at the real thing, but at Alamo Village in Brackettville, 150 miles west of San Antonio.

- The house inhabited by the psychotic cannibal family in *The Texas Chainsaw Massacre* was moved from its original Quick Hill foundation in Austin to Kingsland, about fifty miles northwest. It's now a restaurant at 1010 King Court, and, no, that's not Leatherface minding the grill.

- One-of-a-kind crooner Roy Orbison was born west of Odessa in dinky Wink, where his up-and-down career is celebrated at an eponymous museum on Texas Highway 115. Like fellow Texan Buddy Holly, Orbison was a rock god who made it cool to be a geek.

- South Plains College in Levelland, about thirty miles west of Lubbock, is one of the few institutions where you can get a degree in country music. And Levelland's Mean Woman Grill (209 E. Texas Hwy. 114, Levelland, TX, 806-897-0006) is just the place to scope out future Nashville fodder over Frito pie.

Juárez) in Juárez might just be the best place to hide out and swill margaritas on the planet. If you believe the staff, the margarita was invented on the premises in 1946. (I shook hands with an elderly gentleman who was introduced as the inventor. "Great drink," I told him. He didn't speak English.) And Marilyn Monroe bought the house a round after her divorce from Arthur Miller. (Celebs would often get quickie divorces down here back in the day.) I believe both claims, true or not.

CHILTON

Once upon a time, a Dr. Chilton was at the Lubbock Country Club and wanted a cocktail that offered the proper refreshment from the harsh Panhandle summer. He instructed his bartender to mix the juice of two lemons with a vodka and club soda cocktail, and serve it over ice and with a salted rim. Today Chilton's legacy lives on in the cocktail that bears his name and is widely available in Lubbock's bar scene. Most places skimp and only squeeze one lemon; the Conference Cafe (3216 4th St., Lubbock, TX, 806-747-7766) does the good doctor proud and throttles two.

AUSTIN'S SIXTH STREET

One of the best places to catch a buzz and some live music in the whole country, Sixth Street is definitely the drunkest street in the Lone Star State. Hippies, hipsters, hip-hoppers, and rednecks converge on the seven blocks between I-35 and Congress Avenue, one of the densest clusters of watering holes and music venues anywhere. It's often closed to traffic and user-friendly, with minimal cover charges and relatively cheap drinks. Some say it's past its prime, gotten too much hype for its own good, but it's still a very easy place to accidentally spill a half-dozen Shiner Bocks down your throat.

HUH?

MARFA MYSTERY LIGHTS
U. S. 90, 9 MILES EAST OF MARFA
MARFA, TX

Is it gas? Is it aliens? Ghosts? Or an optical illusion?

It's probably just gas. Between Marfa and Alpine on U.S. Highway 90, you'll see a rest area with an unusual window cut into a solitary outdoor wall. At dark, you'll see why this particular rest area is so deluxe. On the horizon, bulbs of light appear on a nightly basis, then typically do a little dance, brighten a bit, and fade to black. Scientists have yet to come up with an explanation that placates everyone, thus the luminous globs' name: the Marfa *Mystery* Lights.

On some nights, the roadside viewing platform looks like a scene out of *Close Encounters*, loaded with gawkers of all kinds. Other nights it's empty, with only the lights to keep the solitary onlooker company.

JFK CONSPIRACY

The grassy knoll. The magic bullet. The second gunman. The events of November 22, 1963, remain unsettled in the public consciousness. Did Lee Harvey Oswald act alone and assassinate JFK without backing from Castro, the Mob, the Far Right, the Russkies, the Venusians, the Dutch, or even some shadowy corporation? More than forty years later, polls show the majority of Americans reject the Warren Commission's finding that Oswald was indeed the lone gunman.

It happened in Dealey Plaza in downtown Dallas. Oswald's "Sniper's Nest" was on the sixth floor of the Texas School Book Depository (411 Elm St., Dallas, TX, now the Dallas County Administration Building) at the corner of Elm and Houston Streets. The sixth floor houses a museum (214-747-6660) about JFK and his assassination. The grassy knoll is just to the southeast on the north side of Elm Street between the old depository and the underpass.

SUBGENIUS

First I printed out some pages off the Internet. Then I bought *The Book of the SubGenius*. Then *Revelation X*. Somewhere along the line, I realized this stuff wasn't a joke but that these folks were telling the truth and J. R. "Bob" Dobbs was the key to my own happiness and my own maximization of slack. Dang it all if this stuff doesn't work.

We all need more slack. Go to Dallas, go to Austin, go anywhere—wherever you see the opportunity for the most slack.

For more information send $1 to the SubGenius Foundation, P. O. Box 140306, Dallas, TX, 140306 or go to www.subgenius.com. Praise "Bob!"

GRUB

STEAKS, BARBECUE, TEX-MEX

There are three primary food groups in Texas: steaks, barbecue, and Tex-Mex.

Naturally, steaks in Texas have got to be bigger than the steaks anyplace else, and nobody goes bigger than Amarillo's Big Texan (7701 I-40 E, Amarillo, TX, 806-372-6000). As the billboards scream "Eat a 72-ounce steak dinner and get it for free*!" with the asterisk being the price tag if you don't finish it in an hour, $72. I once watched an unhappy Australian fail, but would never want to try it myself. But if you're looking for quality over quantity, check out the Perini Ranch Steakhouse (3002 FM 89, Buffalo Gap, TX, 325-572-3339), fifteen miles south of Abilene in Buffalo Gap.

Barbecue is another culinary religion in the Lone Star State. Everybody has their own particular favorite, and the traditions vary from region to region. Stalwart standouts include Sonny Bryan's in Dallas (2202 Inwood Rd., Dallas, TX, 214-357-7120), Stubb's in Austin (801 Red River St.,

Austin, TX, 512-480-8341), and the Spoon in Lubbock (3604 50th St., Lubbock, TX, 806-792-8544).

Like beef and barbecue, Tex-Mex is something of an art form down here, with many of its true masters calling El Paso home. My mouth waters at the mere thought of the chicken enchiladas at the L & J Café (3622 E. Missouri St., 915-566-8418) or the carne picada at the H & H Car Wash and Coffee Shop (701 E. Yandell Dr., 915-533-1144).

SLEEPS

AUSTIN MOTEL, HOTEL SAN JOSE, THUNDERBIRD

In Austin, you can't find many places more prototypically vintage than the 1938 Austin Motel (1220 S. Congress Ave., Austin, TX, 512-441-1157, www.austinmotel.com). Hipper but pricier, the Hotel San Jose (1316 S. Congress Ave., Austin, TX, 800-574-8897, www.sanjosehotel.com) is from the same era as the Austin Motel, but it got a colorful contemporary facelift in the 1990s. Both places are convenient to Austin's celebrated bats—they swarm out at sundown from their day hang under the Congress Avenue Bridge, a couple of blocks to the north—as well as the celebrated nightlife that follows.

In the more remote West Texas category, the Hotel San Jose's proprietors worked similarly hip wonders with the Thunderbird in Marfa (600 W. San Antonio St., Marfa, TX, 877-729-1984, www.thunderbirdmarfa.com).

MISC.

POOLS

There is no antidote for the stifling Texas summer like a Texas-sized swimming pool. Two of my favorite pools anywhere are spring-fed colossi in the Lone Star State: Barton Springs Pool in Austin and Balmorhea Pool in the middle of freaking nowhere. Barton Springs (2201 Barton Springs Rd., Austin, TX, 512-476-9044) is in Austin's Zilker Park and is 68 degrees Fahrenheit year-round. Balmorhea (9207 TX Hwy. 17 S, Balmorhea, TX, 432-375-2370) is near the tiny West Texas town of the same name and features a classical-looking, 1.75-acre pool that's got diving boards and concrete styling around it but fish and turtles swimming in its rocky depths.

RAMBLE ROAD TRIP HALL OF FAME

WOLFMAN JACK

Legendary DJ Wolfman Jack makes the *Ramble* road trip hall of fame for a road trip he embarked on with a buddy in 1963. Their trip to Del Rio, Texas, involved commandeering what was likely the world's most powerful radio station, XERF across the border in Mexico, in a gunfight, doubling the ad rates for the ministers who preached to the entire world over its airwaves, and—when said ministers refused—debuted crazed, lecherous Wolfman Jack that very night with a lewd joke and a B. B. King record. The ministers paid up the very next day, but Wolfman Jack just moved to a later spot. Jay J. Johnson of Del Rio's super-cool Villa Del Rio B & B (800-995-1887) knows the whole exceedingly odd XERF story, a tale that involves goat testicles, the FCC, and James Brown climbing a radio tower in dress shoes.

SIN AND SALVATION

4 DAYS, 566 MILES, 3 STATES

There he was, staring me right in the eye. His glassy eyes were lifeless; the smoke of countless cigarettes stained his fur coat. I smiled and craned my neck toward him. His name was Buck.

Buck is a dog, a St. Bernard; a dead St. Bernard, to be precise. A dead St. Bernard who weighed about 300 pounds when he was alive. Buck's mounted head hangs on the wall of the Shooting Star Saloon in Huntsville, Utah, just a few miles east of Ogden. The Shooting Star is Utah's oldest bar, serving up sin for roughly 126 years at the time of my visit.

I had eaten lunch in the booth next to Buck an hour before, washing down a Star Burger (two quarter-pound beef patties and a split knockwurst) with a Budweiser draft. I had to cover the meal with an out-of-state check.

Then I drove a few miles to the Abbey of the Holy Trinity, where twenty-two Trappist monks made honey and preserves to cover the costs of dedicating their lives to prayer. "The monks are getting very elderly," an elderly monk at the monastery's gift shop told me. "There's been twenty-two of us for a very long time."

I watched a video about the monastery and opted not to join up and make it twenty-three. That's when I returned to Buck's side. I told the bartender I'd come back because I wanted to take a few pictures. I took Buck's photo. I made sure the bartender wasn't looking. That's when I kissed him.

Before lunch, I stood at the bar as the Shooting Star's owner spoke to a gray-haired man accompanied by a couple of clean-cut guys and a cute girl, all in their twenties.

"I was born in the rock house on the corner seventy-seven years ago," the distinguished elder said. "In my day, if you were an evil young man in Huntsville, you would sneak in the back door of the Shooting Star Saloon and shoot pool."

"Did you?" I asked.

"How do you think I became successful in life?" came his snappy retort.

The cute girl pulled on my sleeve. "I just want you to know," she whispered, "he's a judge at the federal court of

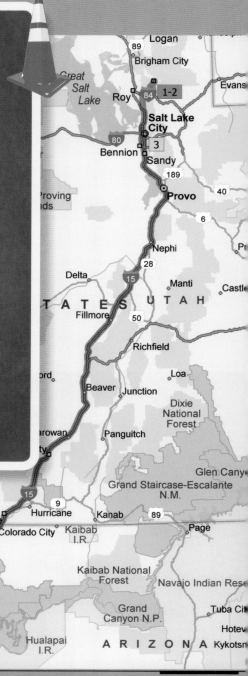

TRIP INFO

1. **Shooting Star Saloon**
   7350 E. 200 S
   Huntsville, UT
   801-745-2002

2. **Abbey of the Holy Trinity**
   1250 S. 9500 E
   Huntsville, UT
   801-745-3784

3. **Temple Square**
   downtown Salt Lake City, UT
   800-537-9703
   www.visittemplesquare.com

4. **Lady Luck Casino**
   206 N. 3rd St.
   Las Vegas, NV
   800-634-6580
   www.ladylucklv.com

5. **Double Down Saloon**
   4640 Paradise Rd.
   Las Vegas, NV
   702-791-5775
   www.doubledownsaloon.com

appeals in Salt Lake City. We work for him; he's showing us his hometown." I vainly wracked my mind for a good line to flirt with the pretty young clerk.

Utah's relationship with sin and booze has always been rocky. Drunkenness was a big issue even before Hoken Olsen first opened the Shooting Star somewhere around 1879. The 80,000 Mormons who settled here in the 1840s thought that booze was an appliance of the devil then and things haven't changed all that much since.

But it's always been easy enough to get a drink—where there's money, there's booze and all sorts of other sin. Olsen ran a thriving moonshine operation in these parts during Prohibition. There isn't a dry county in Utah today, although you have to plunk down $4 for a membership to drink at a "private club," which in most every other place is just a bar.

Me, I'm no stranger to bars or booze. I'm an inveterate sinner in many a Utahn's eyes because I'll drink and smoke weed and curse and do all sorts of other terrible things. I don't go to church on Sundays and never really have. I doubt I'd ever get out of bed if it weren't for coffee.

Gluttony might well be my deadliest sin. I can't control it sometimes, and indulge in midnight snacks of candy and bowls of cereal and chips and salsa. On the plus side, I've gotten better at ignoring the easy allure of food and shed fifty pounds in the process. And I don't smoke cigarettes anymore, don't gamble, and am typically, as luck would have it, celibate. You can get a buzz by resisting temptation. And resisting it can even become as addictive as giving in.

After my brief interlude with Buck, I headed south to posh Park City. As I drove, I thought about the monastery's video and what it described as "the three basic questions of life:" Where did I come from? What am I doing with my life? Where am I going?

I also thought of the toilet seat that hung on the inside of the men's room door at the Shooting Star and the accompanying sign that read, "Ladies' Toilet Seat—10 Cents a Sniff—Honor System."

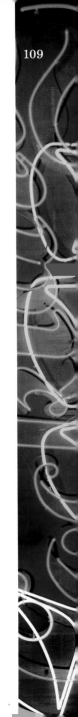

But any headway on answering life's key questions was interrupted by a night hopping around Park City's watering holes. My guide from the Park City tourism bureau wrote a *Sex in the City*-style column for the local alternative paper.

"The rest of the state calls Park City 'Sin City,'" she said. "In Utah, sin is what we've done tonight—drink a bottle of wine with dinner."

At the end of the night I lamely failed to verbalize a suggestion for some sort of sinful rendezvous.

I went to bed just a few hours before the elderly monks at the Abbey of the Holy Trinity got up. Their ascetic lifestyle calls for a 3:15 a.m. wakeup and seven or so chants and prayers and other religious rites every day, not to mention a vegetarian diet—with the lone exception of the annual Founder's Day Feast in July, at which the monks gorge on Kentucky Fried Chicken in their once-a-year give-in to sin.

Hangover in head, I went about the next day, eventually working my way to downtown Salt Lake City, where with dinner I again imbibed more alcohol than necessary. I later resisted the temptation to go out and get drunker but instead gave in to the temptation to doze on my hotel room's couch and inhale a sack of Jelly Bellies from the honor bar.

I woke up fully rested and contacted a pair of beer buddies from high school— Bobby and Mark—and wrangled them into lunch at a Mexican joint called the Red Iguana and the grand tour of the Mormon Temple in downtown Salt Lake City.

The Red Iguana specializes in the Mexican sauces known as mole, so I ordered the Mole Amarillo, with chicken, almonds, and guajillo and habanero peppers. It was spicy enough to make me sweat. And make me wonder if eating spicy food was a sin according to any religious doctrine. If it is, they'd surely look at me like I was slaughtering a kitten as I worked my way through this particular meal.

We had a second round of beers and paid our check, and drove back to the city's ornate centerpiece: Temple Square. Bobby and Mark were quite reluctant, being resident gentiles in Mormon country.

"If you would have told me I was going to be at Temple Square today when I woke up this morning, I wouldn't have believed you," said Mark. "But I didn't think I'd end up in jail tonight, either."

I told him that I saw Mormonism as *the* American religion, the most success-ful homegrown faith by far. I told them that there were more Mormons than Jews, 3,800-year head start notwith-standing. It's like baseball or apple pie, I said, only with an unusual mythology involving dark-skinned Lamanites and light-skinned Nephites and the North American Jesus. Personally, I eat it up: I'm fascinated, disgusted, and amused by the success of the Latter-day Saints (LDS), all at once. But I'm not big on any other organized religion, either.

We wandered around in front of the Mormon Temple, where several wedding parties

were ogling happy new husbands and wives. But entry into the temple is strictly relegated to church members; lacking the proper credentials, we could not go in. Mark talked about making a break for it and bull rushing the door. He also said he'd heard that both the bride and groom's private parts got blessed during a Mormon wedding.

Instead of trying to bust inside, we wandered over to a fountain where a tour group was originating. A pair of young female missionaries, one from France and one from Indonesia, spoke about Joseph Smith and his visions.

"The greatest thing in history happened in the 1820s," said the French one. "God the father and the son appeared to the boy Joseph Smith and told him that he was to restore that church that Jesus Christ established himself."

Our guides started leading us to the next stop on the tour. I began to follow, with Mark and Bobby dragging their heels behind me, then spotted another pair of Mormons— one Finnish, the other from Maryland (Sister Stephenson)— and decided to swap guides.

"Is it a sin to switch tour groups because the Mormon tour guides are better looking?" I asked my cohorts. They weren't sure. I guess we'll find out in the afterlife.

After describing the laborious-yet-glorious, forty-year construction of the Mormon Temple, our new guides stopped at the monument to the seagulls that ate the locusts that threatened Salt Lake City's crops in 1848, and then they

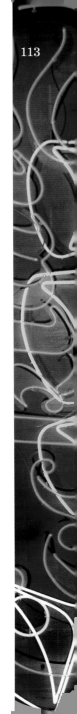

took us into a visitor center and up to an oversized statue of Christ under a dome decorated with murals of the cosmos.

A recording of a booming male voice, presumably that of Jesus himself, began to play. A baby's piercing cry almost immediately overpowered the recording. Jesus talked about the creation of Earth and dying on the cross and that sort of thing.

I sat there, dubious of the whole thing. But Sister Stephenson looked good in her pink sweater vest. She made it clear that her devotion to Jesus was the most important thing in her life.

"By the way," Mark whispered, "I was just kidding about ending up in jail tonight."

After leaving the enormous statue of Christ, we were led to the final stop: a small movie theater where we were shown a brief film that detailed Jesus' post-resurrection visit to North America and all the healing he did for the various natives. There was no dialogue in any language whatsoever.

We were given cards and pens to furnish the church with our names, addresses, phone numbers, and email addresses— as well as any comments we might have for the LDS Church. I filled in my name and email and the comment, "Keep up the good work." I looked at Mark's card. He filled in a fake name, as had Bobby, along with the note: "Nice church."

We handed Sister Stephenson and the Finnish Mormon our cards as we exited. They saw the weakness in my heart from a mile away and started harping on me to provide more information—namely my address and phone number.

I hesitated. Bobby and Mark briskly walked to the escalator.

I swear Sister Stephenson gave me a sinful vibe. I'm sure she didn't mean it that way.

I couldn't help it: I gave them my address, but not my phone number. I'm sure some missionary will see that card as a strong lead someday and ring my door. I'm hoping that I'm not home when they do.

We drove from sleepy downtown to the even sleepier Salt Lake suburbs Bobby calls home. According to Bobby and

Mark, boob jobs and speeding are too prevalent in metro SLC to be sinful in the eyes of the LDS Church. But booze is still definitely on the sin side of the ledger. We stopped for a six-pack of Provo Girl at a gas station, a local micro-brew that has generated quite a bit of controversy with its provocative billboards. (Provo is known as the state's most devout city.)

I left for Vegas in the morning. As I drove through the Utah desert, I had some very deep thoughts. What is sin? Does it feel better to give into temptation than resist? Will that Twinkie be the difference between heaven and hell? That crack rock? That teenage transvestite hooker?

I've heard Utahns eat more ice cream and Jell-O per capita than the residents of any other state. But is it any worse to drink a beer than eat an ice cream cone? How about ten beers versus ten ice cream cones? What would Buddha and Jesus and Joseph Smith do?

Sure, I've had quite a bit of trouble knowing when to say when with booze, but once you get bit by so many bad hang-overs and make an ass of yourself so many times, it's easier to resist the stuff. But sweets and junk food are a much more insidious sin, where the resulting punishment creeps up on you. If I'm bored and it's late, I have to fight the urge to consume whatever junk food is available. Otherwise, the next thing you know, you've got hypertension and weigh 300 pounds.

But, yes, I've found that there is indeed enlightenment in resisting that midnight ham sandwich. There are also times when those Hot Tamales are screaming at me so loud that I drive to 7-11 for a big box and make short work of them before nodding off on the couch.

Enough about midnight snacks. Those three questions posed by the video at the Abbey of the Holy Trinity—Where did I come from? What am I doing with my life? Where am I going?—again took over my thoughts.

Quasi-hypnotized by the passing red rock along I-15, no easy answers again came to mind. I do know that I'm not too sure about the state of religion these days. It seems too many people nowadays use their faith as a tool of puffing up their own ego and looking down on those who don't share their beliefs. This is contrary to the fact that virtually every religion agrees that ego and vanity must be sublimated to humility in order to find inner peace, enlightenment, Zen, heaven, you name it.

And I've always been wary of people who look to a singular idol as their calling in life, their one true thing, and dismiss all others, whether that idol is Jesus Christ or snowboarding or indie rock or money. I think every deity would agree that balance is key to the divine life, not over-whelming focus on one little aspect. But I also think that finding that one true thing can help put together the rest of life's pieces in the proper proportions.

What is my one true thing? I'm not sure I have one. I'm not sure I should care.

I rolled into Vegas in the late afternoon and got a $35 room downtown at the Lady Luck Casino. On the way back to my car to get my bags, I thought about grab-bing one of the free booklets detailing the area's thriving escort industry but real-ized someone was walking behind me so I did not. But on my way out of the parking garage, a somewhat homely, middle-aged couple was pe-rusing the same booklets. Sin gets more and more mainstream by the year.

I had a beer while watching a parade of sex-crime stories on the local news then realized I'd left something in my car. Somehow my passenger-side door was slightly ajar. The backseat of the Saturn was a complete disaster—a briefcase, a bookbag full of books and CDs, jackets, all sorts of crap. But nothing was missing.

When I got back in the lobby, a group of thirty Koreans with big suitcases had taken over the hotel's elevator infrastructure, so I ran up thirteen flights to my room, unable to wait. The round trip took thirteen minutes in all. Uh-oh. Could Lady Luck (the demigoddess, not the hotel) be telling me something?

After Pat O'Brien, *Entertainment Tonight* was on the tube. Paris Hilton allegedly had sex with Mary-Kate Olsen's boyfriend. I put on a nice shirt my mom had given me and hit the town.

Vegas is surreal and synthetic and excessive and everybody is at least slightly askew—myself included. This is where debauched men lose their retirement plans in an evening. This is where used-up women pass out at slot machines after trying to solicit passersby for $20 blowjobs. This is the gaudiest jewel of human stupidity and greed and indulgence in the world, first (temporarily) settled by Mormons in 1855 combing the desert sand for iron to cast into bullets and Native Paiutes to convert into Saints. The

ore for the former was too impure, leading Brigham Young to pull out of the area after just two years.

The Mafia came the next century, and today's mind-boggling resorts mushroomed under the watch of Corporate America over the last twenty years. As of 2005, seventeen of the twenty largest hotels in the world were within a few miles of each other on the fabled Strip.

After my descent on the elevator, stop number one was the ATM in the Lady Luck lobby, where $5 in fees got me $100 in cash, the first $100 bill I'd ever gotten from an ATM, to be exact.

Then came the dinner buffet at Fitzgeralds's. For $9.95 plus tax, I stuffed myself: Plate one was peel-and-eat shrimp, rice pilaf, tater-crusted cod, and a few pepperoncini. Plate two was baked ziti, green beans, and a buttered roll. I continued to push myself, ordering a Budweiser to go with my vanilla non-fat yogurt and brownie. The meal came to a screeching halt with my second

dessert—a piece of dry chocolate cake that tasted more like flour than chocolate.

I thought food might be my sin, but something kept me from going too overboard with it. Booze remained another story.

I moved to the bar and slid a $20 bill into the video poker. I don't even like to gamble, but figured I would do it for the sake of research. I took my time and milked two or three comp drinks out of it, listening to the karaoke in the adjacent bar.

I hate losing money. After sliding $13 in the hole, I cashed out.

But the night wore on. I made way through a $5 beer at Caesar's, and a Royal Flush that won me $64 at O'Shea's across the street. Flush with money, I took a cab to the Double Down Saloon. This dive is the perfect contrast to the glitz of the

strip, every inch of it covered in psychedelically disturbing murals, with punk and metal bands gracing its stage. It never closes.

I had a beer and a couple of shots of Ass Juice ($3 apiece, three for $11). "I'd like some information about the $20 puke insurance," I asked the bartender, pointing to a sign on the wall and yelling at the top of my lungs over the British thrash band on the stage. It went downhill from there.

A White Russian at the Hard Rock. A Bulgarian cabbie. I'm not sure exactly what time I got back to my room at the Lady Luck.

Hungover the next morning, I thought I might still be about even from the $64 quarter at O'Shea's. No such luck: I was $49 in the hole. That one $100 bill had evolved into a twenty, two fives, and twenty-one ones.

I looked through my notes, three increasingly sloppy receipts that were the work of a golf pencil and a bender: "I [heart] Mormon Pussy"—a bumper sticker on the wall of the Double Down. "Sickly Sweet Marg"—a reference to a bad margarita experience at Fitzgerald's. "Lost $12—make that $13."

I was wearing my underwear and a $7 shirt bearing the word "BEERZONE" above the slogan "CHAOS IN THE U. S. A."

I hoped I'd have some sort of orgasmic spiritual revelation at an all-you-can-eat buffet, but it actually came while pounding away on the keyboard on this very story. I typed, hungover in the morning sun on the sixteenth floor of the Lady Luck, and realized that moment was in itself enlightenment, my one big thing: writing and traveling. Typing in a strange hotel room is as close as I get to a religious ritual.

I thought back to the three key questions of life and quickly answered them. (I was hungry and needed to get it over with.)

Where did I come from? My family—where else? What am I doing with my life? I'm driving all over the country seeing as much as I can before the snow starts to fall, writing. (About 18,000 miles down in four months, about 6,000 miles to go in the next five weeks.)

And I know exactly where I'm going: Downstairs for the beckoning breakfast buffet, then the Liberace Museum across town.

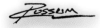

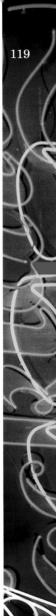

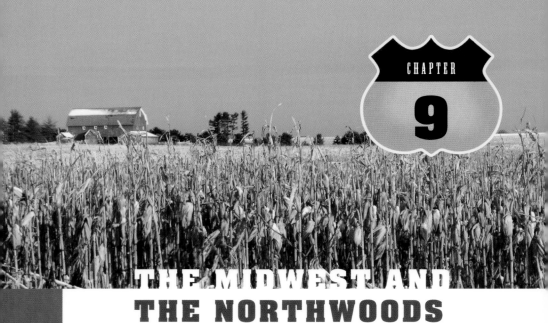

THE MIDWEST AND THE NORTHWOODS

The Midwest, which was of course the West before the West was the West, is in the middle of the country both geographically and culturally. Playing in Peoria is part of the game around here. Even in Ohio, the conduit between back East and the Midwest, blandness is something of an art form.

The population center of the Midwest is Chicago. It's also the region's commercial and cultural capital, and one of the country's truly great cities. But why its founders decided to build such a terrific city where the weather is so awful is beyond comprehension.

Outside of Chicago, it seems like there's something of a skyscraper envy permeating Midwestern culture. Because the buildings of the smaller cities can't match up to the skylines back East, and the mountains don't quite measure up to the ones out West, the region had to manufacture its own greatness—in the form of giant presidential faces, giant Paul Bunyans, giant turtles, giant Vikings, giant fish, and giant et cetera.

ILLINOIS (POP.12,713,600)
- Chicago gave the world its first Twinkie, McDonald's, color TV, and atomic reactor that generated electricity.

INDIANA (POP. 6,237,600)
- With the state motto, "Crossroads of America," Indiana has more interstate per square mile and more interstate intersections than any other state.

IOWA (POP. 2,954,500)
- More than 90 percent of Iowa can support crops, with about 25 percent of the nation's best topsoil within its borders.

MICHIGAN (POP. 10,112,600)
- Michigan has more shoreline than any other state except Alaska, and the world's longest freshwater shoreline.

MINNESOTA (POP. 5,101,000)
- Minnesota's nickname—"Land of 10,000 Lakes"—is somewhat modest. There are 11,842 lakes of more than ten surface acres in the state.

MISSOURI (POP. 5,754,600)
- The 1904 Louisiana Purchase Exposition in St. Louis was the site where the world was introduced to hot dogs, iced tea, and ice cream cones.

NEBRASKA (POP. 1,747,200)
- Lincoln's fifty-nine-mile "O" Street is said to be the longest main street in the country.

NORTH DAKOTA (POP. 634,000)

SOUTH DAKOTA (POP. 770,900)
- After President Benjamin Harrison signed North Dakota and South Dakota into statehood on November 2, 1889, he wouldn't tell anyone which bill he inked first. Thus, it's a mystery to this day as to which state was the nation's 39th and which was the 40th.

OHIO (POP. 11,459,000)
- Cleveland boasts the nation's oldest traffic light. Drivers have been running it since 1914.

WISCONSIN (POP. 5,509,000)
- Wisconsin makes more than 2 billion pounds of cheese a year, about a quarter of all domestic fromage, but the state has fallen off to number ten in beer production after leading the pack a century ago.

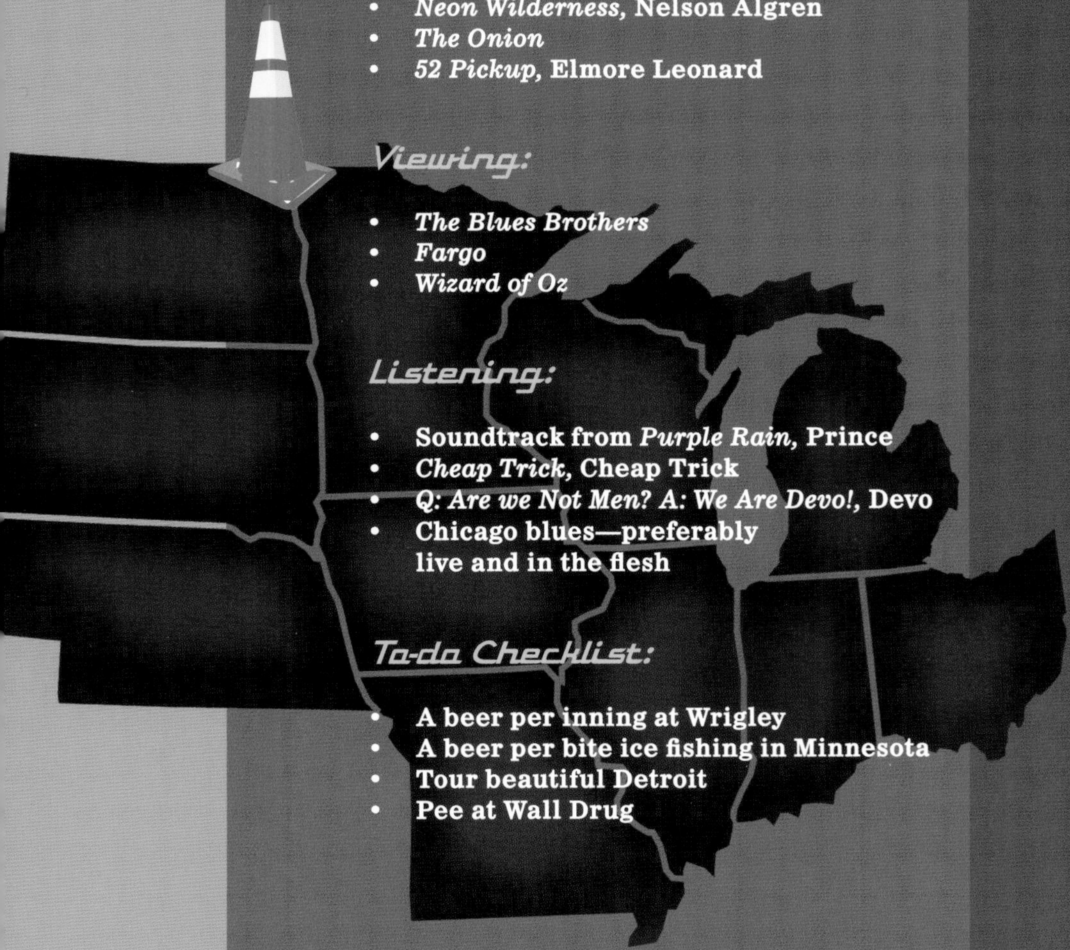

123

Reading:

- *Neon Wilderness*, Nelson Algren
- *The Onion*
- *52 Pickup*, Elmore Leonard

Viewing:

- *The Blues Brothers*
- *Fargo*
- *Wizard of Oz*

Listening:

- Soundtrack from *Purple Rain*, Prince
- *Cheap Trick*, Cheap Trick
- *Q: Are we Not Men? A: We Are Devo!*, Devo
- Chicago blues—preferably live and in the flesh

To-do Checklist:

- A beer per inning at Wrigley
- A beer per bite ice fishing in Minnesota
- Tour beautiful Detroit
- Pee at Wall Drug

After the land of 10,000 lakes gives way to the Great Plains to the south and the west, the culture tends to nudge a bit to the right. In Kansas, the battle is over evolution and creationism in the classroom, and it's easy to see why God has such a strong grasp on the Sunflower State: The scene is fairly nice if a bit bland, but no matter who you are, a tornado can materialize out of nowhere and destroy your house at any given moment. That's why it's best to just fear God and not ask too many questions in these parts.

BIG THINGS AND OTHER ROAD ART

HEARTLAND OF ROAD ART

It seems that every last town in Wisconsin, Minnesota, and the Dakotas has its own world's largest something or, failing that, its own resident self-taught artist whose life's work is on proud display in his yard. Some towns are lucky enough to have both.

In Minnesota, there are big Paul Bunyans in Bemidji and Brainerd, the world's largest floating loon in Virginia, Big Ole the Viking in Alexandria, the world's largest ear of

corn in Olivia, a big Jolly Green Giant in Blue Earth, and Chisolm's Iron Man, the third-largest freestanding sculpture in the United States, bested only by the St. Louis Arch and Lady Liberty.

Wisconsin has outsider folk art that outshines even its cheesemaking. The Forevertron in North Freedom is the enigmatic 400-ton creation of one Dr. Evermor, who plans to ride the thing into outer space. Fred Smith's Concrete Park and Herman Rusch's Prairie Moon Sculpture Garden are lifelong works of public outsider art. And the 140-foot fish at the National Fresh Water Fishing Hall of Fame in Hayward is another worthy diversion.

Then you've got the Dakotas, in some respects grand champions of big roadside art.

SoDak got things rolling with Mount Rushmore, which paved the way for the ambitious Crazy Horse Memorial, potentially a work in progress forevermore.

NoDak gamely responded with the world's largest cow (New Salem) and the world's largest buffalo. Former schoolteacher Gary Greff's Enchanted Highway between Gladstone and Regent in Hettinger County, North Dakota, might be the last word, with six—and counting—installations, including the big *Tin Family*, the enormous *Grasshoppers in the Field*, and the gigantic *Pheasants on the Prairie*.

BERWYN ART MALL
7043 CERMAK RD.
BERWYN, IL
708-344-9242

Cermak Plaza is no ordinary aging suburban shopping mall. Okay, it is, but it's also a gallery for some of the most unusual public art masterworks in the country. Start with Dustin Shuler's *Spindle*, nine cars impaled on a big nail, and *Pinto Pelt*, a Ford Pinto's cladding splayed out like a bearskin rug; George Rhoads' whimsical breeze-powered *Windamajig*; and Barry Miller's *Moon Bells*, which you can play with the affixed mallet.

CARHENGE
NE HWY. 87, 2.5 MILES NORTH
ALLIANCE, NE
WWW.CARHENGE.COM

Stonehenge is an enigma. Built some 4,000 years ago, the famed structure on England's Salisbury Plain has yet to be comprehensively explained. Exactly how a nomadic population managed to transport dozens of thirty- and forty-ton stones and painstakingly fashion them into an elevated ring will likely remain a mystery.

Carhenge, on the other hand, is not quite so baffling. A replica of Stonehenge in terms of size and orientation, it took shape on the western Nebraska plains fifteen years ago, with junked American cars in place of the slabs of stone. Building Carhenge, according to creator Jim Reinders, was, "something to do at our family reunion."

Built on the family farm during the summer of 1987, the construction involved seven days of work and a lot of cold beer. With the help of a backhoe and a forklift, Reinders and a dozen relatives positioned thirty-eight cars (including several classic Cadillacs, an AMC Gremlin, and a Willys pickup) in accordance with Stonehenge's modern appearance. Then they painted the cars battleship gray.

"Carhenge and Stonehenge were built for the same reason," said Reinders. Stonehenge, "has been a burial spot, a place of worship," he continues. "Some people say it was built for navigating the stars, but I think that's baloney. I think the builders said, 'Hey, baby, we were here. We lived a life. This is a monument to our time on earth.'"

Ditto, said Reinders, for Carhenge.

GARDEN OF EDEN

Sᴏᴜᴛʜ ᴏꜰ KS 18
Lᴜᴄᴀs, KS
785-525-6395
www.garden-of-eden-lucas-kansas.com

Samuel P. Dinsmoor marched to the beat of his own drummer. A Civil War veteran who fought for the North and a card-carrying Populist, Dinsmoor was also a devout Christian, a Mason, and a Social Darwinist. He started building his home—a cabin made of interlocking limestone "logs"—in 1907 and didn't stop for twenty-two years. The house is surrounded by more than 100 of Dinsmoor's cement sculptures; his subjects range from crucified workingmen to Adam and Eve to the all-seeing Masonic eye.

Operating the Garden of Eden as a tourist attraction, Dinsmoor outlived his first wife and married for a second time in 1924. At the time, he was eighty-one—in other words, sixty-one years older than his twenty-year-old bride. They had two kids together, the younger of whom was the youngest surviving child of a Civil War vet as of 2005.

Dinsmoor was self-taught and dedicated to his craft. He used 2,273 sacks of cement in his statues and dubbed his place "the most unique home, for living or dead, on earth." Of course, a viewing of his mummified corpse—permanently housed in the mausoleum out back—is part of the Garden of Eden tour.

W'EEL TURTLE
ND Hwy. 3
DUNSEITH, ND

Not a lot happens in Dunseith, North Dakota. Big rigs roar by on North Dakota Highway 3 on their way to and from warehouses on both sides of the border. Sometimes a truck breaks down; sometimes one loses a wheel.

The latter has happened at least 2,000 times, it would seem, because that's how many rims went into W'eel. A monument to recycling and salvage, W'eel is a forty-foot turtle with a one-ton head, made entirely of tire rims welded together by George Gottbreht in 1982. The subject is a tribute to the nearby rolling greenery of the Turtle Mountains.

BIG VAN GOGH
JUST NORTH OF I-70, EXIT 17
GOODLAND, KS

Defying explanation beyond the connection between its sunflower subjects and Kansas' "Sunflower State" nickname, there is a giant easel with an equally giant reproduction of one of Vincent van Gogh's sunflower paintings on a vacant lot in Goodland, Kansas. It's actually a hand-painted reproduction, the work of Canadian artist Cameron Cross, who has actually spearheaded three such projects. The first "Big Easel" went up in Cross' native Manitoba in 1998, an Australian counterpart in Queensland followed in 1999, and Goodland installed its van Gogh in 2001. The paintings—which require more than a month of ten- to twelve-hour days—measure about twenty-three feet by thirty-three feet and their easels exceed eighty feet in height. Cross hopes to find communities interested in the other four paintings in van Gogh's sunflower series, but no takers have emerged after the initial four-year rush.

R. I. P.

WILLIAM S. BURROUGHS, JR., 1914–1997
Bellefontaine Cemetery
4947 W. Florissant Ave.
St. Louis, MO

The scion of the family who invented the adding machine, William S. Burroughs, Jr., was one of the staunchest contrarians who ever walked the planet. If the mainstream and masses were going for it, Burroughs seemed to think it must be poison. His frank writing covered his heroin addiction, his homosexuality, and his visions of a surreal urban landscape where talking bugs and bizarre drugs were the norm.

Immortalized as Old Bull in *On the Road*, Burroughs was also something of a twisted mentor to Jack Kerouac, as well as Allen Ginsberg and other notables of the Beat Generation. But Burroughs transcended the beats in both his writing and his lifestyle, which included a stint on the lam in Mexico after he shot his wife in the forehead playing a drunken game of William Tell.

Burroughs also invented his own medium: the cut-up. Long before the days of Microsoft Word, he would bang out a few pages on his typewriter, indiscriminately slice and dice them, glue them back together in random order, and re-type the story. The method didn't make for the most accessible prose, but Burroughs' cut-ups couldn't be called dull either.

The cut-up, from Burroughs' point of view, was a way to get past one's most inflexible mindsets and see the world in a new light. He thought you could even peer into the future with the right cut-up and, presumably, a big pile of drugs.

Trivia Box:

- Prince, a Minneapolis native, runs his empire from Paisley Park Studios at 7801 Audubon Road in suburban Chanhassen. Renowned club First Avenue was used as a location in *Purple Rain*.

- Jake and Elwood Blues' derelict hotel under Chicago's 'El' train is long gone, but the spot of *The Blues Brothers'* finale, the Richard J. Daley Center, is still there at 118 N. Clark Street.

- Ferris Bueller spent his day off all over Chicago—the John Hancock Building, Wrigley Field, Dearborn Street, and the Art Institute of Chicago—but Ferris' house is actually in Long Beach, California.

- The Who drummer Keith Moon's infamous twenty-first birthday party in 1967 (which degenerated into a massive cake fight and Moon driving a car into the pool) was held at the Holiday Inn (now a Days Inn) at 2207 W. Bristol Road, in Flint, Michigan.

- Muncie, Indiana, dedicated a downtown alley to Ball State alumnus David Letterman. Dave's Alley is on the 200 Block of S. Walnut Street.

- Underground, autobiographical comics scribe Harvey Pekar maintains a low profile in Cleveland Heights in east metro Cleveland.

Burroughs' longevity was a big slap in the face to the "Just Say No" crowd. For a person to inject, inhale, and otherwise imbibe every psychoactive substance he could lay his hands on and live to the ripe old age of eighty-three ran counter to their propaganda.

JAMES DEAN, 1931–1955
PARK CEMETERY
MAIN ST., NORTH OF TOWN
FAIRMOUNT, IN

Live fast, die young, and leave a good-looking corpse. Well, two out of three isn't bad.

James Dean's star was white-hot after *East of Eden*, landing him the part of Jim Stark in *Rebel Without a Cause*. But Dean never lived to see his defining role onscreen, killed when he smashed his Porsche into a Ford making a left turn on September 30, 1955. *Rebel* opened a week later. Half a century later, nobody has captured youthful angst quite like Dean did.

His star still burns bright in his boyhood home of Fairmount (pop. 3,500), where fans from all over the world make regular pilgrimages to pay respects to the actor whose image represents the peak of American cool forevermore.

VICE

GREEN MILL
4802 N. Broadway
Chicago, IL
773-878-5552
WWW.GREENMILLJAZZ.COM

The most pitch-perfect jazz club in the country, the Green Mill opened in 1907 and became one of Al Capone's favorite haunts when he was at the Prohibition-fueled peak of his career. Coincidentally or not, the place was also one of my

favorite haunts at the peak of my drinking career at Northwestern University.

But beyond its significance in mobster lore, the Green Mill looks, sounds, and even smells just like a jazz club should, with dinky little booths, Guinness and Schlitz on tap, and not enough light to read but enough to find your drink. And the jazz musicians who grace the stage are some of the country's best.

SAFE HOUSE
779 N. Front St.
Milwaukee, WI
414-271-2007
WWW.SAFE-HOUSE.COM

"International Exports, Ltd.," reads the sign out front. Is this even a bar? You press on. Inside is a woman at a desk in a bookcase-laden office. She asks if you've been followed, then for a password. Are you sure this is a bar?

It is a bar, and one of the country's most original bars at that—once you get past security, that is. Open since the 1960s, the place has spy stuff all over its walls, James Bond movie nights, secret exits, and classified de-programming techniques for soon-to-be brides and grooms.

HEMP FORESTS

The Midwest is home to several wild hemp forests, leftovers from industrial fiber crops that pre-dated the American prohibition of pot—the last legal hemp crop was planted in the Midwest in the late 1950s. These forests are found in Kansas, Missouri, Iowa, Illinois, Minnesota, Indiana, and elsewhere in the country's breadbasket. And yes, they are technically illegal, although the plants don't seem to realize that.

Commonly known as "ditchweed," this stuff is not worth smoking—it has only the tiniest traces of marijuana's active ingredient, THC, as does all industrial hemp. It does, however, make for a good photo opportunity, and would make for even a better cash crop if it were legal—not as an illicit drug, but as a raw material for paper, rope, fabric, and a zillion other things. Almost every other country on the planet has legal hemp agriculture, and it's even been shown to help replenish the soil.

Most of the Midwest's hemp forests are down gravel roads in rural areas. Ask around. Or you can cross the Canadian border into Manitoba and Saskatchewan and see some legal hemp agriculture—and talk to farmers who will tell you it makes for cheaper, better paper and fabric than any wood on the planet.

REPLAY LOUNGE
10TH AND MASSACHUSETTS STS.
LAWRENCE, KS
303-749-7676
WWW.REPLAYLOUNGE.COM

Likely the hippest bar in Kansas, the Replay Lounge might be the only watering hole with pinball-themed décor in the country—including a killer mural and several light fixtures—and five good pinball machines to boot. Live indie-rock bands, DJs, and a jukebox all offer good musical diversions, and usually not what you'd expect. There's a large, interesting outdoor area with booths and powerful heaters that skirt Lawrence's smoking ban.

HUH?

GREAT APE TRUST OF IOWA
4200 SE 44TH AVE.
5 MILES SOUTH OF DES MOINES, IA
WWW.GREATAPETRUST.ORG

The bonobos will not be seeing you today.

The minds behind the Great Ape Trust of Iowa built a home for eight bonobos (sometimes called pygmy chimpanzee) to live as self-sufficiently as possible. The bonobos control everything. They can activate the waterfall on their splash pool. They exchange items with humans through slots that connect to walkways. Most importantly of all, only invited guests may observe the bonobos—they have a closed-circuit view of the entry and can pick and choose exactly whom they let in.

Right now that's only researchers, but ordinary folks may soon have a chance to visit the house and be turned away by a monkey; check the website for up-to-date information.

LEILA'S HAIR MUSEUM
815 W. 23RD ST.
INDEPENDENCE, MO
816-252-4247

Leila Cohoon, founder of the Independence College of Cosmetology, has collected items made out of human hair for years. Her museum showcases these unusual works of art—more than 150 wreaths and thousands of pieces of jewelry made at least in part from shorn locks.

No, these things are not the result of a creepy ritual or anything like that. The wreaths are actually the product of a Victorian-era tradition. Families would intertwine their hair into meticulously woven masterpieces. While human hair art is not as big as it was in the eighteenth century, Cohoon and company do their best to interest a new generation in haircraft. They've got their work cut out for them.

THE HOUSE ON THE ROCK
SPRING GREEN, WI
608-935-3639
WWW.THEHOUSEONTHEROCK.COM

The house on Deer Shelter Rock is an architectural oddity par excellence. The longtime project of Alex Jordan, The House on the Rock started out as a vacation home that parodied Frank Lloyd Wright's Taliesin, but it snowballed in many different directions over the years. The fourteen-room house is now the centerpiece of a sprawling attraction that has numerous buildings variously occupied by knights' armor, dollhouses, weapons, a miniature circus, and a giant organ.

But all of this is just a distraction from the amazing house itself, with all sorts of quirks and crannies: a 375-foot-ramp to the entrance, a three-story bookcase, a bronze statuary, indoor waterfalls, and the Infinity Room, which juts out more than 200 feet above the forest floor ten stories below, and has 3,264 windows to take it all in.

GRUB

FRIED CHEESE CURDS

Wisconsin fairs—not to mention the arteries of fair-goers—would not be the same without the glorious but humble fried cheese curd. The recipe is pretty simple: Get some cheese curds, slather them in egg batter, and deep-fat fry them. The result tastes much better than it reads.

The best cheese curds are served by remote Wisconsin bowling alleys. The state's best just might be doled out at Dyckesville Bowl (6426 Sturgeon Bay Rd., 920-866-9846) in Luxemburg.

LOOSE MEAT SANDWICHES
WWW.MAID-RITE.COM

Iowa's contribution to world cuisine, the loose meat sandwich, is pretty much like a sloppy joe, only not so sloppy or a hamburger, except much more diffuse. They're the sandwich "too good to be a patty," according to the Maid-Rite Corporation, the prime purveyor of loose meat sandwiches. In other words, there's no patty at all—the ground beef is cooked loose. There are about 100 Maid-Rite locations scattered throughout the Midwest, most of them in Iowa.

CINCINNATI CHILI
WWW.SKYLINECHILI.COM

Cincinnati, Ohio, is said to have more chili parlors per capita than any other city on the planet. And their specialty is not like the bean-heavy chili you find most everyplace else. Inspired by a Greek stew, a Macedonian immigrant named Tom Kiradjieff conceived of Cincinnati chili in the 1920s. He replaced lamb with ground beef, kept the cinnamon and cloves, and added chili powder and other spices. It's thinner than other chilis and more often viewed as a topping rather than a meal in itself.

It's still served just like Kiradjieff did it: Two-way is chili on a spaghetti bed, three-way is two-way with shredded cheddar on top, four-way adds red beans or diced onions, and five-way has both beans and onions on top of everything else. You can also get it poured on fries, hot dogs, and just about anything else.

Skyline Chili is the Queen City's biggest chili chain, but they are far from alone.

MOTO

945 W. FULTON ST.
CHICAGO, IL
312-491-0058
WWW.MOTORESTAURANT.COM

Food, science, and art collide on the tables at Chicago's Moto. A wait staff clad in black lab coats explains the day's offerings, which might include syringes filled with soup or prosciutto cotton candy. Or sushi that only has an image of a fish printed in food-based ink and no real fish at all. Or a puréed Caesar salad frozen into a cube with liquid nitrogen. Or carbonated salsa. Some courses are described on the menu with the words, "there are no words to describe this course." The menus, made from potato starch, are also edible.

Despite its unique culinary approach, the critics agree: Moto's food tastes real good. Executive Chef Homaro Cantu has fun playing with food—and he wants his patrons to do the same.

TRAVELERS CLUB INTERNATIONAL RESTAURANT & TUBA MUSEUM

2138 HAMILTON RD.
OKEMOS, MI
517-349-1701
WWW.TRAVELERSTUBA.COM

Typically, one has to venture into two establishments to eat and gander at a tuba collection, but in Okemos, Michigan, these two tasks can be thankfully accomplished under one roof. Serving a menu that veers from cheeseburgers to stir-fry to burritos to gyros, the restaurant also has specials from a different region of the world every month. The Tuba Museum is the result of one of the proprietors' tuba playing; tubas of every size and shape hang from the walls as gracefully as a tuba can.

AMERICAN SIDESHOW

2,100 MILES, 5 DAYS, 13 STATES

When I was a kid, I developed a fixation on human oddities and the sideshow. I drew cartoon versions of Chang and Eng Bunker, the original conjoined Siamese twins, when I was about ten. I read their biography, *The Two*, somewhere around that time. Their true story struck me as more compelling than any fiction.

Giving rise to the international superstar, the American sideshow and its kin left an unmistakable mark on the country's culture. And like the sitcoms of today, the sideshow provided a human mirror for the audience to peer into and reaffirm its normalcy by looking at people similar to them—or else those who were clearly far less normal.

But the line between normal and abnormal is a subjective thing, and there are people who dismiss the mainstream and intentionally plant themselves a little beyond the normal border—or a lot.

I set off on my journey into the dark heart of the American celebrity on a Tuesday in July 2005, driving around Boston to Middleborough, on the heel of Cape Cod. Founded in 1669 and Massachusetts' second-largest city in terms of land area, Middleborough is perhaps best known for something on the other side of the size spectrum: little people. It's the hometown of Lavinia Warren, better known as Mrs. Tom Thumb. Her husband, General Tom Thumb, was from Bridgeport, Connecticut, also the home of one Phineas T. Barnum, who discovered the little guy in 1842 when Thumb was just four years old.

The Thumbs resided in a mini-mansion here in the mid-1800s when they weren't touring the world. Their life stories are told at my first stop, the Middleborough Historical Museum, which has a collection of photographs, personal effects, and advertisements.

Barnum initially paid Thumb $3 a week, about what his father earned as a carpenter. It soon became $50, thanks to Thumb's super-sized charisma. By the 1850s, General Tom Thumb was one of the first superstars at the dawn of mass media. His 1863 wedding to Lavinia was a media spectacle—engineered by Barnum, who wanted to sell tickets to the event.

142

CANADA
ONT.

Rochester • Syracuse • VT. N.H.
Grand Rapids Lansing
MICHIGAN • Detroit • Erie Buffalo NEW YORK Albany MASS.
Toledo Cleveland Hartford CONN R.
ayne PENNSYLVANIA Altoona New York [2]
bus Akron Pittsburgh Harrisburg N.J. [3]
Columbus
[4]
Baltimore Dover
WEST VIRGINIA [5] DEL.
Charleston Washington, D.C.
Beckley Richmond Virginia Beach
V I R G I N I A Hampton
[6] Greensboro
ville Raleigh
Charlotte NORTH
TH CAROLI
RLINA Columbia
Savannah
Jacksonville
Orlando
Tampa [8]
[7]

TRIP INFO

1. **MIDDLEBOROUGH HISTORICAL MUSEUM**
18 JACKSON ST.
MIDDLEBOROUGH, MA
508-947-1969

2. **BARNUM MUSEUM**
820 MAIN ST.
BRIDGEPORT, CT
203-331-1104
WWW.BARNUM-MUSEUM.ORG

3. **CONEY ISLAND: SIDESHOWS BY THE SEASHORE**
WEST 12TH ST. AT SURF AVE.
BROOKLYN, NY
718-372-5159
WWW.CONEYISLAND.COM

4. **MÜTTER MUSEUM**
19 S. 22ND ST., EXT. 242
PHILADELPHIA, PA
215-563-3737
WWW.COLLPHYPHIL.ORG

5. **AMERICAN DIME MUSEUM**
1808 MARYLAND AVE.
BALTIMORE, MD
410-230-0263
WWW.DIMEMUSEUM.COM

6. **CHANG AND ENG BUNKER'S GRAVE**
WHITE PLAINS
BAPTIST CHURCH
OLD HWY. 601
MT. AIRY, NC

7. **RINGLING MUSEUM OF ART**
5401 BAY SHORE RD.
SARASOTA, FL
941-359-5700
WWW.RINGLING.ORG

8. **SHOWTOWN U. S. A.**
7001 MOTTIE RD.
GIBSONTON, FL
813-677-5443

Today it's a totally different story. Dot Thayer, museum director, told me that most visitors today, "don't realize he was a real person. It's partially because his name comes from a fairy tale. But they are real." And because he went into show business at such a young age, Thumb "really missed his childhood," Dot added.

A display 100 miles down I-95 at the Barnum Museum in Bridgeport, Connecticut, cemented this concept: "Like a living Peter Pan, Tom Thumb seemed to bridge the gap between man and boy—to be a clever child who refused to grow up." Any fading modern-day megastar come to mind?

Another analogy to a twentieth-century celebrity: Barnum was the Colonel Parker to Thumb's Elvis—the thirty-five-inch-tall celebrity gave 50 percent of his earnings to Barnum, and did so even after he went into business for himself. (Elvis gave 25 percent of his earnings to Parker until his death at—like Thumb—age forty-five, at which his estate picked up the tab.) In both relationships, the star saw the promoter as the creator of his career, and in many ways the shrewdly brilliant Barnum was exactly that.

After his father died in 1825 (when P. T. was just fifteen), he went into the grocery business and soon had his own store. His experience hocking everything from raisins to pocketknives gave him a keen sense of what the public wanted and the power of promotion and advertising.

In 1835, Barnum's grocery career went on the back burner when he jumped into the "curiosities" industry with the purchase of Joice Heth, a slave who claimed to be the 161-year-old former nurse of George Washington. After talking down the price from $3,000, Barnum paid $1,000 for Heth, immediately emancipated her, and started booking appearances.

Advertisements claimed that Heth was born in Madagascar in 1674. She apparently didn't look a day over

155 and regaled sellout crowds of stories of her "dear little George." When she died, an autopsy revealed Heth was only about eighty.

But, to paraphrase Barnum, there was a fresh sucker coming into the world every minute. The advances of the Industrial Age meant that for the first time a lot of these suckers had spare money and free time, and the American entertainment business was born. Barnum led the charge and made gobs and gobs of cash in the process. By the 1850s, Barnum was one of the richest men in the country.

I asked the museum's curator, Kathleen Maher, about Barnum's legacy. She didn't hesitate. "Advertising—it's promotion and it's advertising," she said. "He had such an acute sense of what the public wanted. He turned it into a tangible product that he could sell."

Barnum didn't focus on the physical extremes of fat ladies and dog-faced boys, Maher told me, as he promoted everything from ballerinas to wild animals. He coined the phrase "show business," invented the beauty pageant and family entertainment, and opened the country's first public aquarium. His human oddity superstars remain famous today, but he was also showcasing foreigners in their native dress.

"Today we call that EPCOT," Maher said. "P. T. Barnum gets a bad rap. His stuff was more vaudevillian—he never did anything that really maligned anybody. His motto was actually 'instructive entertainment.'"

The ballerina has evolved into an artist, foreign cultures have become more familiar, and animals continue to perform at circuses to this day, but the sideshow's human oddities have pretty much disappeared. Regardless, they're lodged in the country's collective consciousness and in many ways the predecessor of Jerry Springer, *Fear Factor*, and Marilyn Manson.

Trying to get back on the highway, Bridgeport struck me as ragged and jagged around the edges. I was offered crack at a gas station, but politely declined and found the on-ramp to the last leg into the Big Apple, landing in Brooklyn in just over an hour.

Right off the bat I got some bad news: My old friend Barnes was sick as a dog so he would not be accompanying me to Florida. The next day I got more bad news: Because of "severe weather"—i. e., 90 degrees and overcast, with a hint of rain—my third stop, Sideshows by the Seashore in Coney Island, had shut down for the day. My trip would not include performances by Insectivora and "America's young-est female swordswallower."

At first, I was a bit mad that they shut it down when the weather felt more mild than severe. But talking to the side-show's driving force, Dick Zigun, I realized just how far the sideshow had plummeted from Barnum's day in terms of its ability to turn a profit. "Nowadays, sideshows are a good way to lose money," said Zigun after giving me a tour of his empty building. "If we were open today, we would have negative cash flow." (Saturdays are the best day to catch the Coney Island Sideshow, rain or shine, he told me.)

Zigun, a Bridgeport native like his "patron saint" Barnum, told me the modern thrill ride can entertain 1,000 people an

hour or more with two unskilled workers; a sideshow is much more labor-intensive. "It's all about money," he said.

With Barnes laid up on his couch, my college pal Devon had gladly braved the subway ride to Coney Island. (We rode the so-decrepit-it's-scary Cyclone before I tracked down Zigun.) Devon seemed to think the sideshow's shutdown was a fatal blow to my travelogue. I argued that it didn't matter—it helped make a point about the economics of the sideshow, and so on. "It's actually better this way," I lied, envisioning Insectivora gobbling a grasshopper in my mind's eye. Devon looked skeptical.

While rain might have stopped the sideshow, my road trip needed to go on. I patiently cursed while waiting in line for the Holland Tunnel at six thirty that evening, and made my way into New Jersey, which served as a staging ground to visit the Mütter Museum at the College of Physicians of Philadelphia the next day.

The Mütter is a medical museum that dates back to 1858, with a wall of skulls, glass jars containing specimens of all kinds, and a case with the skeletons of a dwarf, a giant, and an average-sized person. This was also the site of Chang and Eng's autopsy in 1874, and a plaster cast of their conjoined torsos and their actual conjoined livers are on display.

The Bunkers would have been separated without hesitation if modern technology were available in their day, said Anna Dhody, collections manager, but it wasn't. "You can die from a nick on the liver," she said. Separating them "would have been very risky." Chang died a few hours before Eng, who was rumored to have perished from fright. Dhody argued that Chang's congealing blood circulating into Eng was more likely the culprit.

The twins were very different, she added. "Chang liked to drink, and Eng was a teetotaler. But Eng liked to stay up late playing poker."

The sight of an abnormally large dried penis in a case behind Dhody was a bit unnerving, but she seemed completely at ease with it, and her relaxed monologue made the Mütter's subject matter seem completely normal. As the museum's PR guy previously told me on the telephone, "Normality is not a black-and-white thing," as he asked me not to include the Mütter in this particular travelogue. (I got his point and wrote a separate listing with a non-sideshow bent.)

Dhody left me to my own devices, and I read displays on conjoined twins. Today medical science has physical imperfection against the ropes, and bearded ladies, crawfish boys, and alligator men are quickly fading into a modern-day mythology.

From Philly I zipped down I-95 two hours to Baltimore and the American Dime Museum, a re-creation of a nineteenth-century American museum. Dime museums, so named for the usual price of admission, thrived in the second half of the nineteenth century, exhibiting curiosities that were educational and sensational, scientific and metaphysical, fake and real. With tens of thousands of exhibits, Barnum's American Museum in New York City was the most prominent.

The American Dime Museum's exhibits include wax sculptures of

Abraham Lincoln and 739-pound Daniel Lambert—both were musts for nineteenth-century dime museums—as well as a faux, nine-foot Peruvian mummy (made by a Boston company), authentic taxidermy alongside preserved demons and two-headed grouses, a funhouse mirror, and an exhibit on La Petomane, who "could fart like no one else in the world, before then or since."

Downstairs, a sideshow exhibit includes a mannequin covered with gum, a feathered fish, "The World's Largest Ball O'Ties," and a speaker blaring the pitch of a carnival barker. (I peeked behind the curtain to look at the sound's source and saw little beyond a kitty litter box.) There was also a great group shot of the Ringling Brothers and Barnum & Bailey's sideshow performers from 1933, including albino twins, a giant, a three-legged man, and many more.

"The very early museums displayed human oddities as works of nature," the museum's proprietor, Dick Horne, told me before I left. "Seventy-five years ago, you could either sit at home or you could go out with other people under similar circumstances, exhibit yourself, and make a lot of money. They were the best-paid people on the carnival lot.

"The human oddities didn't feel they were being exploited," he added. "They actually felt whoever was dumb enough to pay a dollar to look at them was the one being exploited. Today we look at it differently."

After finagling my way out of Baltimore and through Washington, D. C.'s thorny rush hour, I drove into the night with the North in my rear-view mirror and the South quickly unspooling before me. It struck me that the North and South were not unlike Chang and Eng—Thai for "left" and "right"—joined near the heart, sharing the same lifeblood, so different yet so alike.

After 400 or so miles, I made it to a friend's house in Greensboro, North Carolina, shortly after dark and enjoyed leftovers, conversation, and cold beer until midnight, at which point I fell soundly asleep in the eighth different bed in twelve nights. As I drifted off, my friend's comment—"You've got to write about yourself and how the journey changed you"—echoed between my ears.

After breakfast and an hour's drive, my first stop the following morning was the cemetery behind the White Plains Baptist Church, the final resting spot for Chang and Eng Bunker and their respective wives. A lawnmower perturbed the otherwise placid scene; I took a few photos and went looking for a restroom.

Just outside Mt. Airy, North Carolina, the Bunkers settled in White Plains to be with their wives, sisters with whom they sired a total of twenty-one kids. They managed this by sticking to a rigorous schedule: Rain or shine, they spent three days at Eng's house and then migrated the mile to Chang's house for three days, a ritual they repeated for years. Born Buddhists and converted Baptists, the Bunkers donated the land for the church in front of their graves and the money to build it.

Interestingly, Chang and Eng's adopted hometown of Mt. Airy is also the hometown of Andy Griffith and served as a model for Mayberry in his eponymous television show. The show's writers really should have used a chapter of local history in their teleplays, perhaps re-imagining Goober and Gomer as conjoined twins.

Nowadays Mt. Airy is as inspired by Mayberry as Mayberry was inspired by Mt. Airy, with such businesses as Opie's Candy and Floyd's Barber Shop and Aunt Bea's Pies. I had lunch with Tanya Jones, Eng's great-great-granddaughter, at Snappy Lunch. I ordered a pork chop sandwich "all the way" and Jones countered with ground steak.

My first question for Jones was: "At the height of their popularity, who was more famous: Andy Griffith or Chang and Eng?"

Jones didn't hesitate. "No question, Chang and Eng. They were known all over the world."

"And what is the moral of the twins' story?"

"Overcoming obstacles," she answered. "They were not going to let anything get them down." Then she noted that she'd been married more than once, and added, "To me, raising a family is a challenge. They raised twenty-one kids with two wives *successfully*."

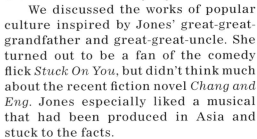

We discussed the works of popular culture inspired by Jones' great-great-grandfather and great-great-uncle. She turned out to be a fan of the comedy flick *Stuck On You*, but didn't think much about the recent fiction novel *Chang and Eng*. Jones especially liked a musical that had been produced in Asia and stuck to the facts.

Jones was in the process of planning the annual Bunker family reunion, a July event that usually draws about 200 people, a small fraction of about 2,000 living descendents of the twins. "There are usually fifteen or twenty [non-relatives] who come to check it out," she added. "Nobody cares. Nobody does a gene-check when you come in."

After a quick photo of the Andy-and-Opie bronze in Mt. Airy, I buckled up for the final leg of the journey: a sweaty, nine-hour drive to Orlando. I located the apartment of yet another college friend: Karlo, a Deadhead physicist who aimed to balance science and partying. On this particular night, however, partying won out.

The next morning, I got up and showered and readied for the drive south to Sarasota and Gibsonton, the final two stops on my 2,000-mile quest. Sarasota is the hometown of the Ringling Brothers who made circus entertainment a science, and now has a museum that bears their name; Gibsonton, a. k. a. Gibtown, is best known as a wintering/retirement town for carnival workers and sideshow performers. Karlo was lollygagging, feeding fish and getting things together, so I told him to meet me at the Gibsonton post office in a couple of hours and hit the road.

I got off of I-75 at the Gibsonton exit an hour or so later and scoped it out. I filled my travel mug with coffee at the twenty-four-hour Giant's Camp Restaurant, so named because it is the last vestige of the businesses founded by Al Tomaini, an 8'4" giant who worked for the Barnum Circus during its glory years. After a drive up and down Gibtown's main drags, I parked at the post office and watched and waited. A group of Spanish-speaking laborers sat in the shade. Traffic barreled by the ice cream stands and bait shops and used car lots.

Gibsonton was a little worse for the wear, but it was also prime real estate, right on the water just twenty miles south of downtown Tampa. In many ways it's a pretty normal place, only one with a history that includes the unsolved murder of the Lobster Boy and the conjoined Hilton twins operating a fruit stand.

Fashionably late and drinking a sixteen-ounce can of beer, Karlo arrived a half-hour later and we went inside the post office, took note of some of the features designed for little people, and made our way to the Ringling Museum in Sarasota, forty miles south of Gibtown. Karlo immediately told me about several run-ins he had with museum security as a teenager, not to mention the various carnal acts he'd engaged in with ex-girlfriends on the museum's grounds.

I had called the museum earlier and they had offered a guided tour, so we went into the security entrance and met the museum's public relations representative. I introduced myself, followed by "my associate," Karlo.

The museum's PR guy was visibly taken aback by Buddha-bellied, bearded, beer-breathed Karlo, and probably wondered what kind of reputable travel writer would bring such an obvious loon out on an

assignment. I paid the PR rep's palpable concern little mind and nodded and smiled my way through a dog-and-pony show before sitting down for a chat.

The circus sideshow died with the big top, I was told. Ringling Brothers erected their last canvas tents in 1957 and moved "The Greatest Show on Earth" into auditoriums and arenas. With that, there was no space for the sideshow.

That night, Karlo and I returned to Gibtown and hit a watering hole called Showtown U. S. A. It was nearly empty. We played darts and had a beer, then took a seat at the bar. Karlo kept up the hasty drinking pace he'd been sticking to since the morning. I was undoubtedly the designated driver.

I asked the bartender about Gibsonton. "It's slow," she said, attributing the bar's lethargy to the fact that this was a carnie town and it was carnie season. "I wish it was busier. That's the way I like it."

Karlo began to hiccup profusely and asked for a glass of water. In between hiccups, he began talking to a woman who had been cleaning up the bar. The woman, Gladys Chase, told us she toured with Ringling as a bearded lady in the 1960s. "But I took shots," she said, and they inhibited her whiskers, but not entirely. She invited us to feel her chin, which had a bit of sandpaper bristle. Despite three years of injections, Gladys still shaved every other day.

I asked Gladys about performing in the sideshow. "I liked it in a way but it wasn't my cup of tea," she said. "When I was doing it, there was money out there. There ain't that much out there right now."

His hiccups cured, Karlo harassed the bartender for another beer. She initially refused, but Karlo wore her down and got himself a bottle of Bud.

I asked Gladys if Gibsonton had changed, and she told me it was growing, with Tampa's suburbs getting closer by the year. Zoning laws that once favored carnies—i. e., ordinances that allowed for people to store rides in their yard during the winter—were falling out of favor as property taxes went through the roof.

"Over on Symmes, we've got 600 to 800 new condo units coming in," sighed Gladys. "And just like everybody else, we're getting a Super Wal-Mart out here."

Soon we wished Gladys well and hit the road. Before heading back to Karlo's grandmother's house in Sarasota, we stopped in at Giant's Camp Restaurant for coffee and what I envisioned to be a snack. Karlo had something else in mind and ordered cheese sticks, chili, and pork chops with hash browns.

I love the guy, but watching Karlo eat was something of a sideshow in itself. As I averted my eyes from the red goo of his hash brown/ketchup/chili disaster, it struck me that Karlo was a far bigger freak than Gladys, and it was by choice.

In the end, I thought to myself, everybody's normal—unless, of course, they don't want to be.

NEW ENGLAND AND THE NORTHEAST

Like a newer, more toxic Europe, the northeastern most chunk of the United States is the cradle of the country, the miniature bed from which this great beast of a nation experienced its most revolutionary growing pains. It's hard to fathom that the country started out as a few colonies of tiny people wearing funny hats.

This is where the country's forefathers built things out of stone and brick and mortar and hard work and craftsmanship. This means things up here were made to last. Unfortunately, it also means that, when somebody made a mistake, it was pretty much permanent. Streets designed for buggies are today clogged with cars. Some $50 seats at Fenway Park are right behind big poles blocking your view of the pitcher, the batter, and pretty much everything else. And let's face it: There are plenty of things in New Jersey begging for a do-over.

But this is where all that history happened. George Washington and the Boston Tea Party and the Revolutionary

CONNECTICUT (POP. 3,503,600)

- Yale students invented the Frisbee in 1920 when they tossed Mrs. Frisbee's pie tins back and forth across the green.

DELAWARE (POP. 830,400)

- Delaware, the first state, is the only state that was claimed by Sweden, Holland, and England.

MAINE (POP. 1,317,300)

- Maine is about the same size as the rest of New England combined.

MARYLAND (POP. 5,558,100)

- The official state sport in Babe Ruth's home state of Maryland is jousting.

MASSACHUSETTS (POP. 6,416,500)

- Massachusetts' Lake Chargoggagogmanchaugagochaubunagungamaug, a. k. a. Lake Webster, has the longest name of any lake in the world.

NEW HAMPSHIRE (POP. 1,299,500)

- In 1934, winds at the peak of New Hampshire's Mount Washington were clocked at 231 miles per hour.

NEW JERSEY (POP. 8,698,900)

- More cars are stolen annually in Newark than in Los Angeles and New York City—combined.

NEW YORK (POP. 19,227,100)

- If Manhattan had the same population density as Alaska, about thirty-five people would live on the thirty-three-square-mile island.

- New York City is about 300 square miles crisscrossed by more than 6,000 miles of streets.

- In 1664, the Big Apple's tallest structure was a two-story windmill.

PENNSYLVANIA (POP. 12,406,300)

- Pennsylvania has more covered bridges and rural residents than any other state, and produces the most sausage, potato chips, pretzels, and mushrooms.

RHODE ISLAND (POP. 1,080,600)

- With a land area of 1,545 square miles, Rhode Island is the size of three Phoenixes.

VERMONT (POP. 621,400)

- With a population around 9,000, Montpelier, Vermont, is the smallest capital city in the country and the only one without a McDonald's within its boundaries.

WASHINGTON, D. C. (POP. 553,500)

- The Smithsonian Institution's National Museum of Natural History in Washington, D. C., has a collection of 126 million artifacts and specimens.

Reading:

- *The Great Gatsby,* F. Scott Fitzgerald
- *Here is New York,* E. B. White
- *The World According to Garp,* John Irving

Viewing:

- *Jaws*
- *Pink Flamingos*
- *The Sopranos*
- Most anything by Martin Scorsese

Listening:

- *Rocket to Russia,* The Ramones
- *Songs for Swinging Lovers,* Frank Sinatra
- *Raising Hell,* Run-DMC
- *Stop Making Sense,* Talking Heads

To-do Checklist:

- Curse a stranger
- Chug maple syrup
- Fish with live eels
- Fuhgedaboutit. No, really. Fuhgedaboutit.

War. The Declaration of Independence. The Constitution. The world's first pink flamingo.

This region is unlike Europe in that its residents have far fewer manners, of course, and bad ones at that. Keep in mind that this is the birthplace of industry—Lowell, Massachusetts, is the world's first industrial city—and where, working fourteen-hour workdays for ridiculously wealthy, mind-bogglingly greedy bosses, time is money. It appears manners bit the dust long ago in favor of painfully blunt but efficient honesty. And time is still money, unless it's time spent cursing, then it's money well fucking spent.

BIG THINGS AND OTHER ROAD ART

MUSEUM OF BAD ART

580 HIGH ST.
(IN THE BASEMENT OF THE DEDHAM COMMUNITY THEATER)
DEDHAM, MA
781-444-6757
WWW.MUSEUMOFBADART.ORG

Just off a clogged rotary southwest of Boston is the town center of Dedham and one of the few institutions on the planet dedicated to championing mediocrity. Whether it boils down to the creating/offending artists' styles, or their choices of subjects or colors, or their "talent," the works that hang on the wall of the Museum of Bad Art are uniformly of a quality that you wouldn't accept on a wall at home. But on the fluorescent-lit walls of MOBA (fittingly next to the men's room in the basement of the Dedham Community Theater), these pieces become enigmatic masterpieces that offer a glimpse into the skewed minds of their creators, and open a Pandora's Box of questions as to their motives, artistic leanings, politics, and mental health.

Which really isn't all that different than the questions that crop up when one views good art. In the end, bad art easily trumps average art, especially when the former category includes such triumphs of the genre as *Sunday on the Pot with George*, *More*, and *Mama and Babe*.

MOBA's permanent collection snowballed over the years. The artists donated some of the pieces; dedicated patrons rescued others from thrift stores, yard sales, and dumpsters. The common thread: There is no denying that all of this stuff is truly bad art. As MOBA Curator Scott Wilson has noted, "You know it when you see it."

LUCY THE ELEPHANT
9200 Atlantic Ave.
Margate, NJ
609-823-6473
WWW.LUCYTHEELEPHANT.ORG

One of the few zoomorphic homes on the planet —animal-shaped houses were more common in the Victorian era, for no apparent reason—this seaside pachyderm was built in 1881 as a functional advertisement for a real estate development south of Atlantic City. The speculators have come and gone and come back again, but Lucy remains, a model home with all the bells and whistles of a normal residence: staircases running up its legs, bedrooms, windows for eyeballs, and a howdah on its back that doubles as an observation deck.

FROG BRIDGE
CT Rt. 661
Willimantic, CT

Thread City Crossing, better known as the Frog Bridge, over the Willimantic River in Willimantic, Connecticut, pays tribute to two totally different things, and one of them is quite odd. The spools are monuments to the thread industry that was the linchpin of the local economy in the 1800s—not odd. The giant bronze frogs on the spools—Willy, Manny, Windy, and Swift—commemorate the "Battle of the Frogs" of 1754, when the noises made by bullfrogs dying of thirst seriously alarmed locals during the thick of the French and Indian War. Locals huddled through the night, thinking it was the Indians coming to get them—very odd.

AMERICAN VISIONARY ART MUSEUM
800 Key Hwy.
Baltimore, MD
410-244-1900
WWW.AVAM.ORG

This terrific museum's mission statement defines visionary art as "art produced by self-taught individuals, usually without formal training, whose works arise from an innate personal vision that revels foremost in the creative act itself."

So what does that mean? Often called outsider art, these are works that the creators often wouldn't even call art. Many of them created pieces now on display at AVAM as a means of self-help or as a substitute for human contact. This is art that makes you look at the world through somebody else's very different eyes. The museum showcases temporary exhibitions with works from many artists that all share a common theme—say, race or addiction, or angels and aliens—as well as works from the museum's 4,000-piece permanent collection.

R. I. P.

JACK KEROUAC, 1922-1969
EDSON CEMETERY
RT. 3A
LOWELL, MA

There's a modest marker for Jack Kerouac near the intersection of Seventh and Lincoln in Edson Cemetery, a couple of miles south of downtown Lowell. Kerouac grew up in Lowell's French-Canadian community, one of many ethnic groups employed by Lowell's once-thriving mill economy.

The mad, Catholic-Buddhist poet of the road spent his childhood in one of the most industrial landscapes on the planet, a downtown dominated by hulking brick textile mills. This tinted his prose, made it naturally cast reflection and description with the artificial as the primary reference point. He yearned for the mythology of the American West, unblemished wilderness, land that couldn't be tamed— thus, the open road.

Modern Lowell echoes with ghosts of industry, echoes of long-since-broken American promises, fading ripples of changing economic and social cycles, seismic shifts of people and technology. Edson Cemetery is mostly quiet, with one side bordering a fairly busy street. Most of those interred here died more than fifty years ago. I'm sure a good deal of them once worked in Lowell's mills, subsisting on pumpkin mush and cheese on bread, living in cramped boardinghouses.

Then there's Kerouac, who left his hometown behind to explore the world beyond, his work bearing the unmistakable mark of a writer reared in a city so at once urban and modern and forlorn and decaying that his hip, post-industrial sensibilities became the template for American cool.

EDGAR ALLAN POE, 1809–1849
Westminster Cemetery
Fayette and Green Sts.
Baltimore, MD

The inventor of the thriller, nobody has done dark and twisted quite like Poe did dark and twisted, not before or since. His short life was marked by insomnia, hard drinking, and borderline madness, and he left a body of work that fit his tortured existence to a tee, deftly capturing paranoia and dread. Every year on Poe's birthday (January 19) since 1949, a masked stranger has showed up at Poe's grave in the middle of the night to leave three roses and a half-quaffed bottle of Cognac. The masked giver—a. k. a. the Poe Toaster—now attracts a crowd of onlookers and garners quite a bit of contemplation about his identity.

MILES DAVIS, 1926–1991
Woodlawn Cemetery
233rd Ave. and Webster St.
The Bronx, NY

A genius of jazz and a bit of a nut otherwise, Miles Davis made music that sounded at once otherworldly and primal. He left us a catalog that includes landmark albums like *Bitches Brew* and *Kind of Blue*, colored by different moods

and textures to the point that even his most extemporaneous tangents feel lived-in.

Davis is buried next to Duke Ellington and Lionel Hampton at the Woodlawn Cemetery in the Bronx, a vast but empty graveyard in the most densely populated city in the country. Beyond this superlative jazz triumvirate, Woodlawn is a who's who of deceased luminaries: Herman Melville, F. W. Woolworth, Irving Berlin, and Joseph Pulitzer are just a few of the notables buried here since the first grave was dug during the Civil War.

ANDY KAUFMAN, 1949–1984
BETH DAVID CEMETERY
300 ELMONT RD.
ELMONT, NY

A hybrid of absurdism and nihilism guided the unusual comedic sensibilities of Andy Kaufman, best known for playing Latka on *Taxi*. While the sitcom earned Kaufman fame, his body of work is as far from television's lowest-common-denominator approach as you can get. He wrestled women, poured drinks on a few patrons' heads, pretty much invented Elvis impersonation, and otherwise merged comedy with conceptual art while simultaneously deconstructing both.

VICE

NYC MAFIA LANDMARKS

Gambino Boss Paul Castellano was gunned down in front of Sparks Steak House on E. 46th Street (212-687-4855) in 1985. Il Cortile in Little Italy (212-226-6060) is the model for Nuovo Vesuvio, Artie Bucco's swanky joint on *The Sopranos*. John Gotti, Lucky Luciano, Paul Gambino, and other Mafia bigshots are buried in Saint John's Cemetery in Queens. Brooklyn's Gowanus Canal is where many Mafia lowlifes sleep with the fishes.

THE UGLY MUG
426 WASHINGTON ST.
CAPE MAY, NJ
609-884-3459

One of the Jersey Shore's longest standing watering holes (est. 1926), the Ugly Mug's ceiling provides the anchor for hundreds of hooks for hundreds of customers' beer mugs. Those facing the Atlantic belong to the club's deceased members. The place also has a great motto: "Mix a little folly with your wisdom. A little nonsense is pleasant now and then."

THE BRICKSKELLER
1523 22ND ST. NW
WASHINGTON, D. C.
202-293-1885
WWW.THEBRICKSKELLER.COM

A homey neighborhood bar, the Brickskeller's claim to fame is what the proprietors say is the world's longest beer list, with more than 1,000 varieties; bottles are displayed for maximum effect in the coolers on the ground floor. And if you sample too many of them, you can get a room right here. The bar occupies the bottom of a historic hotel.

MCSORLEY'S OLD ALE HOUSE
15 E. 7TH ST.
NEW YORK, NY
212-473-9148

Said to be New York's oldest bar, McSorley's is a bit of a tourist trap, sure, but it's definitely worth two or four beers. Why not one or two? Because beers—light or dark are your choices—are sold by the pair. The place is typically packed, with sawdusted floors, swinging doors, and a potbelly stove that are remnants of a history that dates back to the bar's grand opening in 1854. Since then, everyone from Abraham Lincoln to John Lennon have hoisted a mug here.

HUH?

WILHELM REICH MUSEUM
DODGE POND RD.
RANGELY, ME
207-864-3443
WWW.WILHELMREICHMUSEUM.ORG

A physician who was one of Sigmund Freud's top students in the 1920s, Wilhelm Reich parted ways over differing opinions on the nature of the human libido. Freud's line on the libido was initially that it was a natural biological energy akin to an electric charge. Reich took the concept and ran with it. By 1925, Freud changed his stance: The libido was just thoughts and ideas and mental images—there was no actual energy flowing around in people that made them horny.

Reich's research led him to disagree. He felt orgasms were able to release this energy—which he termed "Orgone"—and allow for psychological and physical equilibrium. He demonstrated that humans have a charge at skin level that increased in tandem with pleasure. The psychoanalysis establishment in just about every country in Europe eventually blacklisted Reich.

- Norm! The bar seen in *Cheers* transitions is Cheers Beacon Hill, 84 Beacon Street, Boston, Massachusetts.

- The odd, green statue poking out of the beach at the end of *Planet of the Apes* is located on New York's Ellis Island.

- Monk's Café from *Seinfeld* is actually Tom's Restaurant at 112th and Broadway in Manhattan.

- Ween's Gene and Dean Ween are from New Hope, Pennsylvania, a touristy town on the Delaware River. They played their first gigs at John and Peter's, 96 S. Main Street, 215-862-5981, wwwjohnandpeters.com.

- *The Sopranos'* Bada Bing is in actuality a strip joint called Satin Dolls, 230 Route 17 S., Lodi, New Jersey, 201-909-8983, www.satindollsnj.com.

- The king of trash cinema forevermore, John Waters is a native of Baltimore and has filmed all of his movies there. Pay homage at the Senator Theatre, 5904 York Road, 410-435-8338, www.senator.com. There's even a walk of fame.

- The Ramones played their first show at CBGB in August 1974, 315 Bowery Street, New York, 212-982-4052, www.cbgb.com.

When World War II broke out, Reich made his way to the United States and settled in Maine. It was there—at the research compound he dubbed Orgonon—where he discovered orgone was present in the atmosphere. He sold people orgone accumulators and developed a cloudbuster that he alleged could alter weather patterns by controlling atmospheric orgone. In 1954, the Food and Drug Administration filed a complaint. The FDA said orgone was pure fiction. The judge agreed. Accumulators were dismantled, Reich's publications burned, and Reich himself was incarcerated and died in prison in 1957.

But orgone research lives on at Orgonon, now the home of the Wilhelm Reich Museum and the Orgone Energy Observatory, not to mention a couple of rental cottages.

PHILADELPHIA MUMMERS

WWW.MUMMERS.COM.

Mummery is serious business in Philadelphia. What was born as the pagan Roman ritual *Saturnalias* in 400 B. C. is now the full-time hobby of thousands of otherwise normal plumbers, tough guys, and everyday joes in the City of Brotherly Love. These guys bust their hump on nights and weekends all year to come up with flashy, flamboyant, some might even say flaming clown getups for the annual Mummer's Parade on New Year's Day. Some 15,000 Mummers march in the parade.

Mummers are broken down into different categories—comics, fancies, string bands—and fathers start training their sons to do the Mummers' strut during infancy. A tradition in Philly since 1901, the big parade is now the birthright of hundreds of gangs of clowns. If it's not

New Year's Day, the year-round Mummers Museum (1100 S. 2nd St., Philadelphia, PA, 215-336-3050) is the best place to delve into the rich, weird tradition that is Philadelphia Mummery.

MÜTTER MUSEUM
19 S. 22ND ST.
PHILADELPHIA, PA
215-563-3737, EXT. 242
WWW.COLLPHYPHIL.ORG

In 1858, Dr. Thomas Dent Mütter donated his cache of 2,000 medical specimens and $30,000 to the esteemed College of Physicians of Philadelphia and the museum that bears his name was born.

Now in the mid-1800s, medical science wasn't quite what it is today, so the museum originally displayed jars with preserved organs, skeletons and bones, and all sorts of other specimens you don't see every day.

Over the years, the museum beefed up its collection with such prized specimens as a collection of human skulls (now arranged in a case with placards identifying the cause of death), the skeletons of a giant and a dwarf, the Soap Lady (a nearly unrecognizable body mummified by soap), and the conjoined livers of Chang and Eng Bunker, the original Siamese twins. The organs on display include just about every last hunk of the human anatomy: colons, hearts, brains, genitalia, and so on.

Until the 1970s, almost all of the visitors to the museum were medical types doing research, and only a few thousand a year passed through the doors. But then Gretchen Worden became the museum's executive director, and she promoted the Mütter to the general public with interesting calendars, a coffee table book, and even an appearance on Letterman. Worden, who passed away in 2004, saw the museum's annual attendance mushroom from 3,000 to 60,000 under her watch.

The lesson of the museum: In order for medical science to become what it is today, it had to start somewhere. Preserved wet specimens, skeletons, and other objects that look macabre were invaluable teaching tools at one time. Another lesson: There's a broad spectrum of humanity out there, and there's a lot of gray area when it comes to labeling someone normal or abnormal.

GRUB

SCRAPPLE

The culinary zenith of the Pennsylvania Dutch, scrapple is called scrapple because it sounds a bit more appetizing than fried pork mush. That and because it's made from leftover pig scraps, ground up and mixed with cornmeal, herbs, onions, and pretty much whatever else is on hand. Actually, that description doesn't sound half bad. Keep in mind, however, that scrapple could contain pork skin, pork heart, and pork brains. Typically, scrapple is served with fried eggs and slathered in ketchup, applesauce, butter, or whatever else is on hand.

Try the Red Robin Diner (6330 Frankford Ave., Philadelphia, PA, 215-338-8643), and bring an appetite or do not go at all.

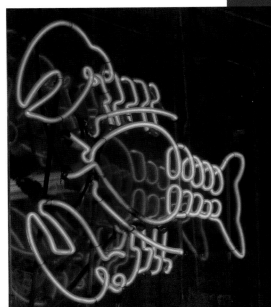

PHILLY CHEESESTEAKS

If scrapple's not your bag, head over to South Street and join the endless debate: Who makes the best Philadelphia cheesesteak?

The Philadelphia cheesesteak is a sandwich of legend. Invented at Pat's Steaks in 1930, real cheesesteaks are beef slathered in cheese (provolone or American will do, but preferably Cheese Whiz), served on a bun, and dripping with grease. The greasier, the better. Just make sure to lean forward while you eat one or you'll ruin your Sunday best.

The famous debate—Geno's or Pat's—refers to the two twenty-four-hour cheesesteak joints on South Street where you'll sometimes wait an hour or more for your sandwich. Other notable challengers include Jim's, Larry's, Sonny's, and a host of other apostrophed men's names.

CLAM CHOWDER

You can't visit the northeastern United States without sampling the clam chowder. But what is the region's authentic chowder? Some recipes call for cream or milk, making the chowder white, while others call for tomatoes, making the chowder red. New England claims the white chowder more often than not, while New York is more often associated with the red. However, both were predated by clear chowder, which emerged as a dietary staple in these parts in the 1600s. Milk and tomatoes were beyond scarce in these times, but clams were anything but, leading early European colonists to whip up colorless chowder as a matter of course. But tomatoes and cream are no longer luxury items, making clear chowder a rarity.

Oddly enough, Rhode Island tradition calls for a pitcher of warm milk to be served with your chowder.

SLEEPS

STARLUX
305 E. Rio Grande Ave.
Wildwood, NJ
609-522-7412
www.thestarlux.com

Wildwood, New Jersey, is known for its mid-century Doo Wop architecture, and this renovated 1951 motel is its crown jewel. With Space Age style to burn, the StarLux is a blast from the past, down to the lava lamps in the rooms and a funky lobby that's got windows for walls and spills out onto the pool deck. If you need more space, get the suite—it's a vintage Airstream trailer.

ANYBODY'S APARTMENT IN NYC

When visiting the Big Apple, avoid the overpriced hotels. Stay at a friend's place. If you don't have a friend in New York, make one on Craigslist, or just rent some random Gothamite's apartment at a site like www.metro-home.com.

RAMBLE ROAD TRIP HALL OF FAME

JACK KEROUAC

On the Road has probably influenced more people to ramble the country than any other book. Fueled by amphetamines and coffee, Jack Kerouac is said to have written his opus about his wanderings in the West in twenty days, to which Truman Capote famously quipped, "That's not writing, that's *type*writing."

But I don't distinguish too much between the two. Kerouac poured his thoughts and experiences into a heady brew of stream-of-consciousness thought and perpetually moving narrative. The book reads like a road trip, never stopping for too long to catch its breath, punctuated by memorably odd characters and spot-on descriptions of places and cities. It made him the voice of a generation, a tag he was never comfortable wearing.

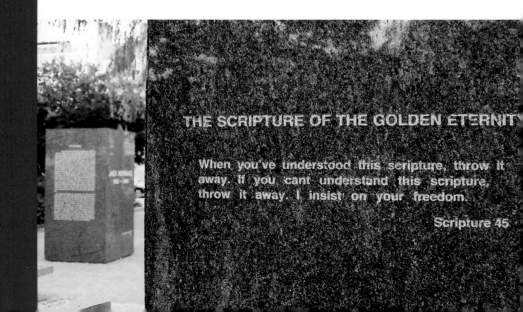

THE SCRIPTURE OF THE GOLDEN ETERNITY

When you've understood this scripture, throw it away. If you cant understand this scripture, throw it away. I insist on your freedom.

Scripture 45

Pay respects to Jean-Luis Lebris de Kerouac at his grave (see " R.I.P." earlier in this chapter) and the memorial in downtown Lowell, Massachusetts, several monoliths of polished granite featuring passages from his books.

CROSSROADS ON LONELY STREET

4 DAYS, 500 MILES, 4 STATES

A warm October night in the Mississippi Delta, the moon was full and tinged with red. I was at the crossroads.

I leaned against my Saturn at the intersection of U. S. Highway 61 and Mississippi Highway 3, quite possibly the fabled spot where Robert Johnson sold his soul to Satan for the ability to play the hell out of a guitar.

And quite possibly not. There is some controversy as to where Johnson's alleged deal with the devil went down. Most blues scholars say it's where U. S. 49 crosses U. S. 61 in Clarksdale, Mississippi, but there's a doughnut place there nowadays—not exactly what I had in mind. But this one fit the bill perfectly.

I stretched my legs after about 500 miles behind the wheel, hoping to circulate blood into my numb buttocks.

There was an acrid smell in the air. Trees were shrouded in mist.

I was alone on the side of the road. Satan was nowhere in sight.

I gave him five more minutes, and then sped off. I still had 100 miles to go until Tupelo, where there was a motel room waiting.

But of course the crossroads is a metaphor, I thought, driving into the night. My stop symbolically cemented this trip as a conscious choice. I could have just as easily taken a different fork at my crossroads. Not that I was going to turn around so close to my goal—the starting point for Elvis Presley.

My foot was firmly on the pedal, the radio set to a Memphis station with DJ Isaac Hayes spinning classic soul. I uncomfortably shifted positions. Trucks roared in the opposite direction. "What if Elvis had taken another path?" I said into my tape recorder. "What was his crossroads?"

I had driven through many crossroads myself leading up to that night, but this had been the only one where I stopped to contemplate. My rambles were winding down for the season and I was ready for a break from the road.

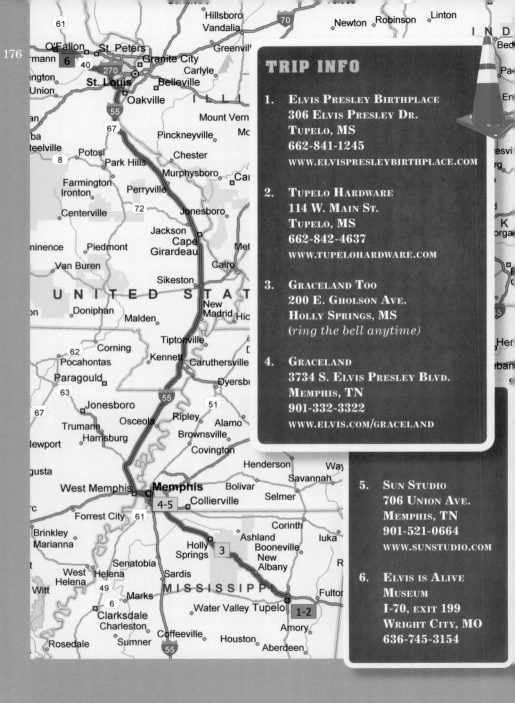

176

TRIP INFO

1. **ELVIS PRESLEY BIRTHPLACE**
   306 ELVIS PRESLEY DR.
   TUPELO, MS
   662-841-1245
   WWW.ELVISPRESLEYBIRTHPLACE.COM

2. **TUPELO HARDWARE**
   114 W. MAIN ST.
   TUPELO, MS
   662-842-4637
   WWW.TUPELOHARDWARE.COM

3. **GRACELAND TOO**
   200 E. GHOLSON AVE.
   HOLLY SPRINGS, MS
   (ring the bell anytime)

4. **GRACELAND**
   3734 S. ELVIS PRESLEY BLVD.
   MEMPHIS, TN
   901-332-3322
   WWW.ELVIS.COM/GRACELAND

5. **SUN STUDIO**
   706 UNION AVE.
   MEMPHIS, TN
   901-521-0664
   WWW.SUNSTUDIO.COM

6. **ELVIS IS ALIVE MUSEUM**
   I-70, EXIT 199
   WRIGHT CITY, MO
   636-745-3154

I'd been driving around the country for fifteen of the previous twenty weeks, covering 22,000 miles and sleeping in fifty different beds in that span. At the time, I was looking forward to the one in Tupelo.

In the room, however, it was quiet and lonely, just me. I drove a couple of miles into downtown Tupelo, parked, and investigated a neon beer sign. The bar was closed. I slowly walked around the block.

Downtown Tupelo was quiet, dead. I ambled toward an old theater across from the courthouse. I saw a girl in a black dress, with black hair and black thigh-high boots, hurrying away. She was alone. Then she was gone into the night.

As I inserted coins into the vending machine at my motel ten minutes later, I watched a lone black beetle crawl across the floor. By the time I'd collected my Starburst, it was scaling the wall next to the machine.

I typed for a while and went to bed.

I woke up late and groggily struggled to pull it together. I checked my email. Nothing pressing. No messages of note on my voicemail, either. Alone on the road had become familiar in its unfamiliarity.

At about eleven o'clock, I made it over to the eastern fringe of Tupelo, Mississippi, where the only sharecropper's shack left behind from the 1920s and 1930s was now the city's claim to fame. On January 8, 1935, in this humble two-room hovel, Gladys Presley gave birth to Elvis Aaron Presley. A twin, Jessie Garon, was stillborn.

Where there was once row after row of shacks, only one remained. When the landowner died, Elvis bought the little house and the surrounding acreage, donating it to the city. The city let it languish until after Elvis died. After fans started making regular pilgrimages, things changed—Elvis' birth house was restored to its 1935 appearance and a museum later opened. I stood face to face with a bronze statue, *Elvis at 13*, and went into the memorial chapel.

It's amazing that people will travel halfway across the world to visit this little shotgun shack. It is akin to a religious pilgrimage, with a gift shop.

I met Linda Elliff of the Tupelo Convention and Visitors Bureau for lunch. A Tupelo native, she was a huge Elvis fan and initially a bit concerned that my focus was on the kitsch, the decline, the peanut butter and banana bloat. I assured her that was not my intentions.

I too have been a big fan of Elvis since I was a kid. Early on, I focused on the jumpsuits and what I then interpreted as 1970s cheese. But now I know better. He had the best rock and roll voice ever, a mind-blowing stage presence, and, sure, the jumpsuits. Shit, he's the King, then, now, forever.

"It was an American dream that he became what he was," said Elliff, "but it was also an American tragedy what happened in the end. If Shakespeare had been alive, he couldn't have written it any better."

Twinless twins, she added, have a unique psychology. The mother clings to the surviving twin more because she knows well how fragile life can be; the child ends up feeling guilty about living when their twin was not so fortunate. Liberace, who inspired Elvis to work Vegas, was also a twinless twin, Elliff said.

It struck me as the opposite of Chang and Eng Bunker: a twin who's never there, rather than the twin who's always there.

I told Elliff about my crossroads experience, applying it to Elvis, bisecting his life into the happy innocent rise to international fame and the second act of dealing with that fame, kicked off by his beloved mother Gladys' death, and concluded by his dogged, druggy descent to an early grave.

She immediately pointed out what she saw as his ultimate peak, the point from which he could go nowhere but down. At twenty-one, Elvis played the Tupelo Fairgrounds on September 26, 1956, and was already the biggest thing to come out of town, ever. Smack-dab in the middle of Elvis' forty-two years, it may well be the most defining moment in Elvis' life, exactly as many fans love to remember him.

While there were many great moments to come, this might also have been the begin-ning of the end: the moment that he became an icon, the moment fame began to become a burden, the shining summit followed by the inevitable downhill slope.

But there were many other crossroads for Elvis. If Jessie Garon hadn't died, maybe he wouldn't have felt as much pressure to perform and make mama proud. If the tornado that devastated down-town Tupelo in 1936 had slightly swerved, it could have easily blown the Presleys' $180 shotgun shack to splinters.

If Gladys had given into eleven-year-old Elvis' desire for a .22 rifle and not helped steer him toward a guitar, maybe Elvis would have been the greatest deer hunter in the tri-state area, still hunting today. And if he hadn't become so rich and famous, maybe he wouldn't have ended up with the colossal pill habit that ultimately killed him.

Linda Elliff took me to Tupelo Hardware, where the aforementioned guitar originated. Apparently, the initial plan was to buy Elvis a bicycle, but the rifle commanded his attention. He begged his mother for the gun, but she would have none of it, and they compromised on a $7.75 guitar. The hardware store still sells guitars to this day. It's the only one I've ever seen that sells promotional T-shirts and guitar picks as well. I picked up a yardstick reading, "Tupelo Hardware: Where Gladys bought her son his first guitar." They couldn't print Elvis or Presley on any of their souvenirs for fear of running afoul of Elvis Presley Enterprises.

Maybe I was at my own personal crossroads that very afternoon. I left Tupelo, realized I was driving on fumes, and cursed to myself as I returned to Tupelo and felt my blood pressure rise.

If I don't get my anger under control, I may look back at that very moment from my deathbed when I'm sixty-four years old, a year before retirement bliss, and wonder: "Why did I let the little things bother me so much? Why did I let my anger, my weakness kill me in the end? Why couldn't I have just gone with the flow?"

I left Tupelo for a second time around three in the afternoon. I stopped seventy miles into the 100-mile drive to Memphis for a quick visit to Holly Springs, Mississippi's Graceland Too.

The house was easy to find. The bright pink paint job, concrete lions, and multihued artificial Christmas trees were dead giveaways.

After ringing the big bell mounted out front, an overweight man with a gray pompadour and sideburns answered: Paul MacLeod, the "#1 Elvis Fan in the Universe," at least according to the homemade poster right inside his foyer.

MacLeod told me dozens of ridiculous things in the span of an hour. He said that a baby feasted on the blood of vigil-keepers killed outside Graceland after Elvis' death. He told me he was locked in the mausoleum with Elvis' body for several hours. He said they had the real story and Graceland and the Smithsonian and the FBI and the KBG (yes, the KBG) were paying them for information.

Paul said he saw Elvis perform in Holly Springs in 1954. "A lady dropped dead right in front of my face," he exclaimed. "I told her, 'Calm down, you're getting too damned excited!' I reached over and shook her, she dropped dead."

Graceland Too is worth billions, MacLeod said. He showed me a picture of a rake and some cash then a whole scrapbook full of rakes and cash and said the place was "raking in the cash."

Sure, Elvis was a self-parody in his later years, but nothing compared to Paul MacLeod, whose mix of nearly unintelligible exaggerations, braggadocio, and other hyperbole was as entertaining as it was disturbing. "This place ought to be declared a national monument," he crowed, "the Taj Mahal of Elvisology, better than Graceland, Disneyland, and Neverland Ranch."

I felt he was a fan who'd lost his idol in his obsession for collecting. His fandom appeared to be more about himself than it

was about Elvis (despite his claims that he would give up his life "right now" to bring Elvis back). MacLeod's crossroads probably came a long time ago, maybe when he named his kid Elvis Aaron Presley or maybe when his ex-wife gave him the ultimatum, "It's me or the Elvis collection," and he told her to get lost. He said he would be buried in the gold lamé suit in the corner, sheathed in clear plastic.

And he would not stop talking. He seemed lonely, which might be why he welcomes visitors twenty-four hours a day, seven days a week.

The drive to Memphis was marked by an impossibly beautiful sunset, a red and orange sky over doggedly blackening forest and meadow.

I checked into a motel a block from Graceland and drove ten miles north to downtown Memphis. The sights reminded me of a college road trip to the city. After a day at Graceland and joking about Elvis kitsch, two cohorts and I were walking and talking and looking for Beale Street.

All of a sudden, a tall, black guy asked us where the hell we were going. We told him, Beale Street, and he told us we were going the wrong direction, straight into a crime-wracked neighborhood where white college kids in Graceland T-shirts might be welcomed with gunfire. After pointing us in the right direction, he introduced himself as Teardrop—he had a teardrop tattooed next to his eye—and told us he had been released from prison the day before.

He said he'd murdered a guy with an ice pick a decade earlier, retaliating for a beating and crack theft. Then he asked for a ride to Chicago. My friend refused. I gave Teardrop $20 and never saw him again.

My previous Memphis trip was also marked by my regret for not spending an extra $6 for the Platinum Tour of Graceland. I skimped and did the Mansion Tour only—no automobile museum, no self-guided plane tours, no Sincerely Elvis Museum. I was going to rectify that mistake this time around.

A few drinks and some Beale Street blues later, I walked back to my car, parked a few blocks away near the former Lorraine Motel, where an assassin's bullet took the life of Martin Luther King, Jr., in 1968. Now the National Civil Rights Museum, I was looking at its neon glow and pulling my keys from my pocket when a black man approached and began telling me about Dr. King's death. He introduced himself as Marvin Louis Booker.

I listened. I even gave him $8 for a leaflet he'd written on Dr. King, which struck me as possibly an unwise investment when he told me he'd been banned from the place during daylight hours. He talked about a conspiracy involving Memphis' white leaders and the FBI and that James Earl Ray was a scapegoat. I bade him goodnight. He asked me for more money.

I drove back down south and got a six-pack of beer at a local convenience store. The place was a little rough around the edges. Then I retreated into my room.

Motel rooms are the most culturally neutral places on the planet. You can be in Anchorage or Iowa or right next door to Graceland and simply pull the blinds, turn on the tube, and forget where you are.

I got up the next morning and drove the block to Graceland. I was still dead set on the Platinum Tour. The damage: exactly $28, exactly one dollar for every year since Elvis' death.

"Elvis sure had a lot of cool cars," I scribbled on a note card in Elvis' car museum. Next door, the Sincerely Elvis Museum was a bit underwhelming and keenly kept the focus off of the sad, last chapter of the King's life, with only one display of his 1970s jumpsuits and a case of the Mountain Valley Water he drank onstage.

Why was—and is—Elvis so huge? His voice, many say (including Paul McLeod at Graceland Too). Chicks loved him, sure—Linda Elliff from the Tupelo tourism bureau told me he was "the most beautiful man ever." He was a regular guy, every boyhood pal said, a good ol' country boy.

But after he was the most celebrated human on the planet, the face of rock and roll started changing and leaving Elvis behind. The British Invasion sucked the wind out of just about every American band's sails.

I got in line for the shuttle to the mansion across the street. An employee gave me the headphones for the audio tour. After disembarking on the other side of Elvis Presley Boulevard, I toured the mansion, scoping the "Jungle Room" and the triple-television arrangement in the TV room, I went out to the racquetball court, which now houses all of Elvis' awards and all sorts of other displays.

I came to an exhibit on the 1968 comeback special broadcast on NBC. Too bad that night wasn't Elvis' midlife crossroads, I thought. At thirty-three, he looked and sounded as good as ever and countered the psychedelic pomposity of the time with black leather and a sneer.

If the special had been Elvis' midlife, he would have lived until 2001 and probably been one of the Traveling Wilburys. But it wasn't, just Elvis' splashy re-entry into live performance that soon snowballed into the Vegas years with all of the pills, erratic behavior, and legendary bad taste. Less than a decade after this stunning performance, he was gone.

I tried to meditate in Graceland's Meditation Garden, right by the graves of Elvis and family. It was leafy, breezy, and serene. I crossed my legs. It wasn't comfortable on the bench. I uncrossed my legs and focused on my breath. Tourists distracted me. A dog in one of the adjacent houses began to bark.

I tried again. A deep breath. Another. Yet another. Very relaxing, this meditation stuff. But meditating on an empty stomach, as Elvis surely learned, is nearly impossible. I needed something to eat, so I pulled myself together and left Graceland without buying a souvenir. I figured my $28 Platinum Tour ticket was souvenir enough.

That afternoon, I toured Sun Studio near downtown Memphis, where Sam Phillips recorded Elvis' first hits. I didn't bring my camera inside, but made sure to slip my Chuck Taylor on the 'X' of black tape that marked the singer's spot—everyone from Elvis to Johnny Cash to David Brookings (my tour guide) had stood here and belted out songs for posterity. Perhaps even more modest and less maintained than Elvis' birth house, the studio—still active and cheap ($75 an hour)—felt like hallowed ground.

I went to the Peabody Hotel at five o'clock for the legendary duck march (overrated) and then explored downtown for an hour, getting a look at the Mississippi River and the architecture as well as Confederate Park and its Jefferson Davis statue.

Another motel room. Dinner alone. I wrote and read and slept.

In the morning, sitting in the third different (but pretty much the same) motel room of the trip, I figured it was time to leave Memphis behind. I really love this city, and all of its history and culture, but it's not my home—at least not right now. I'm a stranger here, and I'm alone. I packed my stuff and left.

Everybody is going to have their crossroads. I'll have mine, you'll have yours, as did Marvin Louis Booker, Paul McLeod, and Teardrop. Elvis had his in 1956, when he came back to Tupelo a conquering hero. He was the hillbilly kid who always wore overalls. The poor sharecropper's kid who wanted a gun but got a guitar. Then suddenly he was onstage driving the girls crazy at the very fair he used to sneak into as a kid, on his way to becoming the world's first and foremost rock star and the biggest musical sensation the world had ever seen.

Yes, Elvis' story is like something Shakespeare would have written—only with a better soundtrack.

I drove about 300 miles north and west to Wright City, Missouri's Elvis is Alive Museum. Proprietor Bill Beeny was one of the high priests of the revisionist splinter sect of Elvis devotees who insisted he had faked his death and was indeed alive. The whole "Elvis is Alive" phenomenon had always struck me as the American analog of the resurrection.

And what better American messiah than Elvis, a hunk of burning American postwar cool, a walking, breathing cultural salvo in the early Cold War. Elvis was so American it hurts. From his commercialism and his rags-to-riches story to his religion and his hypocritical position against illegal drugs, Elvis was emblematic of all that is good, bad, and indifferent about the United States. Most importantly of all, the guy knew how to rock.

Maybe that's why folks like Bill Beeny can't seem to let go. His museum consisted primarily of a few piles of indecipherable "FBI files" and about twenty hanging folders with photocopies of Elvis' will, the transcript from an "Elvis is Alive" episode of *A Current Affair*, and photocopies of newspaper articles about the museum. There was also a half-ass Elvis dummy in a coffin and a bad re-creation of his grave. I wasn't convinced.

Beeny had written several pamphlets explaining his views on Elvis, as well as a book. I rubbed one of many stacks of the latter; my fingertips came back covered in dust. He was also selling homemade tapes and pamphlets with creationist dogma and framed needlepoint pictures of flowers for $1.50. Beeny was far more lucid than Paul McLeod, but he seemed more interested in surfing the Internet than talking to me.

It looked like the Elvis is Alive cult was on the wane.

I bought a $4 pamphlet entitled, "Final proof: The King IS alive!" The book is full of interesting tidbits, and it makes me want to believe that maybe, just maybe, Elvis did go down another road and did not continue down the same dead end of 100 pills a day. To any fan, Elvis faking his death because he was undercover FBI—as Beeny told me—was much preferable to his sordid fate on the Graceland toilet.

I'd like to indulge a different fantasy. Graceland loves to show footage of Elvis playing in the snow. He owned several extravagant fur-rimmed coats that he rarely got to wear—I saw at least two on my tour. He converted a fleet of snowmobiles to "grassmobiles" so the Memphis Mafia could tool around Graceland without any of the white stuff.

Near the bitter end, Elvis had taken an interest in my home state of Colorado. He'd fly to Denver for haircuts and sandwiches at a moment's notice. He'd go to a now-shuttered restaurant for a dish called the Fool's Gold Loaf: a hollow loaf of Italian bread filled with layers of peanut butter, jelly, and bacon. He vacationed in Vail in 1976 and was said to be thinking about buying some property there.

Could that have been Elvis' lost crossroads? If he bought a place in the Rockies in 1976, maybe, just maybe he would have had an epiphany. He would have abandoned his grueling tour schedule and his prescriptions and all of his other demons for the crisp mountain air. He would have lived into his eighties. He'd still be alive now.

My original plan was to cap my Elvis trip with a marathon drive to Las Vegas. Sitting in a motel in Lawrence, Kansas, I found myself at another crossroads. I had just gone to Vegas (see "Sin and Salvation") a couple of weeks prior and ended up with a hangover that lasted two days. The 500-mile drive back to my Denver home loomed. As Buddhist philosopher Lao Tzu has been translated, "The good traveler has no fixed plans."

Fuck Vegas. I decided to go home for another stab at meditation.

THE SOUTH

The South is an easy target. Yes, it's got its problems. That ugly slavery thing, for one. The humble redneck culture, sure, and all of the baggage that comes with it. And gobs and gobs of fried foods.

Yes, the South is definitely a little backwards—okay, a lot backwards—but it's taking baby steps forward, or at least in a different direction. Alabama recently removed the interracial marriage ban from its state constitution, just 157 years after Massachusetts did the same thing. The government now pays North Carolina farmers not to grow tobacco. Most importantly, Arkansas-based Wal-Mart is slowly but surely taking over the world.

Beyond all of its warts, however, the South has got a lot going for it. The food, with all of its butter and spice and tradition and vegetables, you can't get anywhere else. The multicultural stew, the rich tapestry of different cultures and traditions coming together and creating something new. The lush green humid beauty of it all.

But mind your Ps and Qs. Southerners have been known to put down their Bibles and pick up their shotguns if you

ALABAMA (POP. 4,530,200)
- Hitler's typewriter is on display at the Hall of History in Bessemer, Alabama.

ARKANSAS (POP. 2,753,600)
- As of this writing, Bentonville-based Wal-Mart had about 1.3 million employees in the United States.

FLORIDA (POP. 17,397,200)
- Key West, Florida, has had an average temperature of 78 degrees Fahrenheit for the past thirty years—the highest average temperature in the country.

GEORGIA (POP. 8,829,400)
- "The Chicken Capital of the World," Gainesville has a law on the books prohibiting the use of a fork and knife while eating fried chicken.

KENTUCKY (POP. 4,145,900)
- A full 90 percent of the world's Bourbon is distilled in Kentucky.

LOUISIANA (POP. 4,515,800)
- Sure, Texas' is bigger, but the Louisiana State Capitol in Baton Rouge is the tallest in the country at thirty-four stories (450 feet).

MISSISSIPPI (POP. 2,903,000)

- The Mississippi towns of Greenwood, Belzoni, Vardaman, and Greenville, respectively, are known as the cotton, catfish, sweet potato, and towboat capitals of the world.

NORTH CAROLINA (POP. 8,541,200)

- Fayetteville saw two of the greatest moments in sports history: Babe Ruth's first professional home run and the opening of the world's first miniature golf course.

SOUTH CAROLINA (POP. 4,198,000)

- South Carolina was known as "The Iodine State" before adopting its current "Palmetto State" nickname.

TENNESSEE (POP. 5,901,000)

- The biggest earthquake in United States history rattled northwestern Tennessee in December 1811, causing tidal waves on the Mississippi River and shaking church bells in Boston, about 1,000 miles away.

VIRGINIA (POP. 7,459,800)

- The Pentagon in Arlington, Virginia, has more than 6 million square feet of floor space, making it the world's largest office building. It has about 700 drinking fountains and 4,200 clocks.

WEST VIRGINIA (POP. 1,815,400)

- Marlinton has hosted the Roadkill Cook-Off since it began in 1991. Despite its name, the organizers would rather the main ingredients be examples of species found dead on the road and not actual specimens found dead on the road.

Reading:

- Snopes trilogy, William Faulkner
- *A Confederacy of Dunces,*
  John Kennedy Toole
- *Collected Short Stories,* Flannery O'Connor

Viewing:

- *Sling Blade*
- *Gone with the Wind*
- *Deliverance*

Listening:

- Anything by Robert Johnson,
  Elvis Presley, or Al Green
- *Fables of the Reconstruction,* R. E. M.
- Some things by the Allman Brothers
  and Lynyrd Skynyrd

To-do Checklist:

- Stew some roadkill
- Have a dream
- Watch out for gators and snakes
- And have a doctor look at that rash

push them too far. Keep the conversation light, about, say, the intricacies of intelligent design or the stifling weather, and you'll do just fine.

BIG THINGS AND OTHER ROAD ART

PASAQUAN
EDDIE MARTIN RD.
JUST NORTHWEST OF BUENA VISTA, GA
229-649-9444
WWW.PASAQUAN.COM

In the 1930s, Eddie Owens Martin, a New York hipster wracked by a bad fever, had the first of many visions. Three tall figures told Martin of "a place where the past, the present, the future, and everything else all come together." That place was Pasaquan.

The figures explained to Martin that it was his duty to show people that the future could be a peaceful, beautiful place. Then Eddie Owens Martin as the world had known him disappeared. In his place stood St. EOM, the only Pasaquoyan of the twentieth century.

St. EOM left New York in 1957 and returned to his place of birth (and unhappy childhood as the "different" son of a sharecropper), Marion County, Georgia. He spent the next thirty years of his life creating Pasaquan and soothsaying for those who sought visions of their future. He started with an 1880s farmhouse and built it into an elaborate, colorful citadel with more than 15,000 square feet of his murals complemented by all sorts of funky details in all sorts of media. Pasaquan is a true revelation, a work of creative vision melding Native American and African traditions with St. EOM's visions of that special place.

"Why I built all this is to have something to identify with," said St. EOM in a 1978 interview. "This society as a whole, I can't identify with. There is no place in it for me ... so I created my own world, my own vision."

Since St. EOM's death in 1986, Pasaquan has been only sporadically open to the public, typically on July 4 (St. EOM's birthday) and the last Saturday of the month, or by appointment.

OBSESSIONS, ER, CASTLES OF THE SUNSHINE STATE: CORAL CASTLE AND SOLOMON'S CASTLE

CORAL CASTLE
28655 S. DIXIE HWY.
HOMESTEAD, FL
305-248-6345
WWW.CORALCASTLE.COM

SOLOMON'S CASTLE
4533 SOLOMON RD.
ONA, FL
863-494-6077
WWW.SOLOMONSCASTLE.COM

In 1913, a Latvian immigrant named Ed Leedskalnin was engaged to a girl named Agnes Scuffs. He was twenty-six, she was sixteen, but they were in love—or so Leedskalnin thought, until the night before the wedding when Scuffs called the whole thing off.

Leedskalnin was devastated. He bounced around from place to place before settling in South Florida, in 1918. Ed still hadn't gotten over Agnes. So he stewed for a few years, then started building the Coral Castle as a monument to his beloved "Sweet Sixteen" out of huge blocks he carved from the beds of coral on his property.

Strange thing about it, he used only hand tools and never had any help. And he was only 5' and 100 pounds. Nonetheless, after thirty years, Leedskalnin, who came from a family of stonemasons, had fashioned more than 1,000 tons of coral into a bizarre psychedelic fortress. Some of the blocks he moved on his own were bigger than those used in Stonehenge or the Great Pyramid of Giza.

Leedskalnin gave people tours for a quarter and sold them odd pamphlets about his scientific "research" into mineral life, magnetic current, cosmic force, and of course his issues with "Sweet Sixteen." Then one day in 1951, Leedskalnin taped a note that read "Going to Hospital" to the door, went to the hospital, and died the next day.

Howard Solomon started his castle about twenty years after Leedskalnin's passing. His Florida castle is clad in printing plates tossed by the local newspaper and serves as Solomon's private residence as well as a tourist attraction/restaurant/B & B. The castle's post-industrial look complements Solomon's day job of found-object sculptor.

Okay, so Solomon's Castle doesn't have the heartbreak of the Coral Castle, except that nobody bought it for $2.5 million when it was recently on the market. But it is big (about 10,000 square feet) and weird. And it has a moat.

MARGARET'S GROCERY AND MARKET
4535 N. Washington St.
Vicksburg, MS

In 1984, Reverend H. D. Dennis told Margaret he'd build her a palace if she married him. She said yes. And he built her a palace.

Well, actually he converted Margaret's Grocery and Market into a palace that's a folk art church, an eclectic collage of Christian messages and multihued brickwork. While it's no longer a market, it's still active, now dispensing messages of non-denominational love and tolerance instead of soda pop and groceries.

The Rev was born in 1916, fought in World War II, and still keeps himself busy on his monument to love.

R. I. P.

HANK WILLIAMS, 1923–1953
Oakwood Annex Cemetery
1304 Upper Wetumpka Rd.
Montgomery, AL

From his inimitable yodel to his early grave, Hank Williams was always ahead of his time. The man known as "the hillbilly Shakespeare" popularized modern country music with forlorn lyrics that captured loneliness as good as anybody's, before or since.

Dead in the backseat of a Cadillac at age twenty-nine, Williams burned out quickly, signing with MGM in 1947 and recording a string of hits before booze and painkillers started taking a serious toll on his health and career. He'd show up drunk for gigs and his personal life fell to pieces. After the Grand Ole Opry fired him in 1952, it was less than a year before Williams met the fate he sang about in "I'll Never Get Out of This World Alive," dying of heart failure while sleeping it off on the way to a gig in Ohio.

Williams is buried next to his first wife in a grave marked by a grand marble monument. The green hillside cemetery is quite a memorable spot to watch a sunset.

DUANE ALLMAN, 1946–1971
ROSE HILL CEMETERY
1091 RIVERSIDE DR.
MACON, GA

"An unfortunate accident"—a motorcycle crash that involved no drugs or citations by the police—claimed the life of the twenty-four-year-old slide guitar phenom just two years after the release of the Allman Brothers Band's first album in 1969. Nicknamed "Skydog," Allman was a musical prodigy who dropped out of high school to focus on the guitar and was soon one of the most in-demand session players in the South.

But Skydog had grander ambitions than being a hired gun, leading to the Allman Brothers Band's genesis in the late 1960s. His influence on the slide guitarists who followed is unmistakable.

Duane Allman is buried next to bandmate Berry Oakley, whose death a year later was also the result of a motorcycle accident, in Rose Hill Cemetery in Macon, Georgia. In the late 1960s, the Allman Brothers Band would jam in this very cemetery, which is where they came up with the tune, "In Memory of Elizabeth Reed," based upon one of the gravestones here. While they never knew Reed—she died in 1935, before Oakley and Allman were born—they've shared the same address for more than thirty years.

CHARLES KURALT, 1934–1997
OLD CHAPEL HILL CEMETERY
UNIVERSITY OF NORTH CAROLINA
CHAPEL HILL, NC

Not many journalists have taken to the road like Charles Kuralt.

A newspaperman in the 1950s who became known for his offbeat human-interest stories, Kuralt migrated to television in the late 1950s and worked as a roving reporter and did four tours covering the conflict in Vietnam before deciding he wanted out of hard news. In 1967, his "On the Road with Charles Kuralt" debuted on the *CBS Evening News.*

Kuralt's bald, pudgy everyman persona and the quirky subjects he covered were an instant hit. Over the course of the next thirteen years, Kuralt filed more than 500 stories from every state in the country, logging more than a million miles in six motorhomes in the process. He stayed off of the interstates, never had much of a definite schedule, and kept total creative control of his segment. Co-workers said they never knew where he was.

Neither did his wife. After he died, it came to light that Kuralt had a thirty-year affair with a Montana woman—that he essentially had two families. But both women agreed that he was a good man and just chalked it up, I assume, to loneliness on the road.

VICE

DISTILLERY TOURS

Most boozehounds agree that the South has mastered the art of liquor. There are three main sauce groups down here, and bourbon is a good place to start. Technically, it's American whiskey made from at least 51 percent corn, aged for at least two years in charred oak barrels, and is no stronger than 125 proof. By law, Kentucky is the only state that can be named on a bottle of the stuff; 90 percent of the world supply is distilled here. Just about every Kentucky distillery offers tours: Maker's Mark in Loretto (www.makersmark.com), Lawrenceburg's Wild Turkey (www.wildturkeybourbon.com), and Jim Beam in Clermont (www.jimbeam.com) are among the biggest attractions.

Next up is Tennessee whiskey, just like Kentucky

bourbon but filtered through no less than ten feet of sugar-maple charcoal, giving it a hint of smoky sweetness. Jack Daniel's in Lynchburg (www.jackdaniels.com) and George Dickel in Tullahoma (www.georgedickel.com) are among the many Tennessee distilleries open for tours.

Completing the trinity of Southern hard booze: moonshine (a.k.a., mountain dew, white lightning, hooch, and—my favorite—popskull). Long a cultural staple in Appalachia, moonshine is fermented corn and/or sugar mash, distilled into a strong drink. Farmers made the stuff long before Prohibition, and even before the federal government started taxing booze. But the tradition has faded in the face of the modern liquor industry; moonshine used to be a cheap way to get your drink on, but it's just as cheap nowadays to just get a bottle at the liquor store. Regardless, there's been a moonshine renaissance in the South, only now it's legitimate, licensed, and legal. Check out West Virginia Distilling Co. in Morgantown (www.mountainmoonshine.com) and Belmont Farms of Culpeper, Virginia (www.viriginiamoonshine.com).

HUH?

UCM MUSEUM
22275 LA Hwy. 36
ABITA SPRINGS, LA
985-892-2624
WWW.UCMMUSUEM.COM

Pronounced "you-see-em, mu-se-um," John Preble's UCM Museum actually stands for something: Unusual Collections and Mini-Town. It stands for something else, too: Preble's commitment to his inspired art—inspired by the *Weekly World News*, Southern folk art, and New Mexico's wonderful Tinkertown in equal measures.

Two large works—Aliens Trashed Our Airstream Trailer (a UFO impaled in a vintage trailer) and the aptly named House of Shards—are among the many attractions; there's also the reptilian canine dogigator, a fishy reptile bassigator, a huge miniature Southern town (including a Mardi Gras parade and a redneck trailer park), and all sorts of Preble's collections (wacky postcards, barbed wire, paint-by-number paintings, and pocket combs, to name a few).

MUSEUM OF EARTH HISTORY
AT HOLY LAND
EUREKA SPRINGS, AR
866-566-3558
WWW.MOEH.ORG

I plunked down my $8.50 admission and was ready to be wowed. A perky, gray-haired woman readied a flashlight and gave me a pair of headphones. Then she pulled back a velvet rope and the tour began.

"In the beginning, there was nothing," said an omnipotent boom of a voice through the headphones, "On the first

Trivia Box:

- On December 5, 1980, George "No Show" Jones didn't show up for "Nashville Loves George Jones Night" at the Exit/In at 2208 Elliston Place in Nashville, Tennessee.

- The charred remains of the cabin in Sam Raimi's *Evil Dead* are located outside of Morristown, Tennessee.

- Lynyrd Skynyrd named itself after tough gym teacher Leonard Skinner at Robert E. Lee Senior High School in Jacksonville, Florida.

- There's a bronze statue of Dolly Parton on the courthouse lawn at 125 Court Avenue in her hometown of Sevierville, Tennessee. Her theme park, Dollywood, is in Pigeon Forge, Tennessee.

- In Brian de Palma's *Scarface*, Tony Montana shot and killed the Colombian chainsaw killer outside their seedy apartment at 728 Ocean Drive in Miami, Florida.

- On April 5, 1980, R. E. M. played their first gig at a now-demolished old St. Mary's Episcopal Church at 394 Oconee Street in Athens, Georgia.

- In 1957, Jerry Lee Lewis married Myra Gale Brown, his thirteen-year-old cousin, at a church that's no longer at the corner of Highway 51 and Holly Springs Street in Hernando, Mississippi.

- (Also see "Crossroads on Lonely Street" for Elvis' Star Maps in the South.)

day, God created the elements of time, space, and light." The perky gray-hair utilized the flashlight to bring my attention to an abstract interpretation of that day. Then the second day and the third day and so on until we got past the initial rumblings and on to the main event: man and all of the other animals, which the voice told me God created on the sixth day.

The hall of abstract creationist art opened up into the first display room, with "museum-quality" reproductions of dinosaur skeletons. A *T-rex* snarled overhead. Other specimens roamed at eye level. In the corner, a mural of a happy couple clad in fig leafs provided a backdrop for a real plastic tree with real plastic fruit. I noticed a reptile with a man's face behind the pair. It looked like a snake with legs.

"I like that one," I said, pointing out the man-reptile to the guide as the omnipotent voice rattled on and on about original sin.

"The Serpent," she solemnly noted. Uh-oh. I just told this woman I liked Satan.

The Museum of Earth History in the United States is bar none the worst natural history museum I've ever seen. Let it be known: I'm not recommending you plunk down $8.50 to check it out. I did it so you don't have to.

Among the exhibits after the Serpent caused Adam and Eve to give into original sin: a volcanic world wracked by volcanoes; Noah leading dinosaurs and every other species two-by-two onto his big boat; the great flood causing every geological phenomena we now see on Earth, from caves to mountains to sedimentary rock; and of course the Tower of Babel, the resulting God-imposed Ice Age, and modern day—the species' last chance to resist sin.

I bought a \$3.99 leaflet about Noah's Ark. It said the boat, 450 feet long and four stories tall, could have housed 50,000 animals for forty days and forty nights.

GRUB

TABASCO® TOUR
SOUTH OF LAFAYETTE VIA U. S. 90
AVERY ISLAND, LA
WWW.TABASCO.COM

"Tabasco® Sauce has three ingredients," said the tour guide in a Southern nasal drone, "red pepper, vinegar, and salt." She pointed at a huge copper vat that was full of Tabasco.

I took a deep breath and my sinuses were suddenly clear. The HQ of Tabasco Pepper Sauce, Avery Island, Louisiana, is a nature preserve with a hot sauce factory. You'll see some gators and nesting birds, and get a tiny bottle of Tabasco as a souvenir—as well as those cleared sinuses.

SOUTHERN BARBECUE

There are regional variations in meat and sauce, but there is great barbecue in every corner of the South. In North Carolina, it's chopped or sliced pig with pepper and vinegar sauce; in Georgia and South Carolina, they use a mustard base. Memphis and vicinity does pulled pork with a sauce of tomato, molasses, and pepper. Every town has a hole-in-the-wall barbecue place—the rattier, the better—and everyone has their favorite rib or sandwich place. It's on par with religion and football in these parts.

Recommended: the original Dreamland in Tuscaloosa, Alabama (5535 15th Ave. E); Natchez, Mississippi's Pig Out Inn (116 S. Canal St., Natchez, MI, 601-442-8050); Memphis' A & R BBQ (1802 Elvis Presley Blvd., 901-774-7444); and many, many more.

SOUL FOOD

Soul food is another must-eat while traveling in the South. Fried chicken, meatloaf, collard greens, sweet potato pie—this is food for people who love food. The Arcade Restaurant (540 S. Main St., Memphis, TN, 901-526-5757), Memphis' oldest eatery, established in 1919, served Elvis back in the day and just about everybody else since. Eschew the Elvis special of a fried peanut butter and banana sandwich with fries in favor of a platter of Southern veggies: fried okra, candied yams, turnip greens, and mashed potatoes with gravy.

Other great soul food joints: Jeems Diner, 425 Howard Street, Greenwood, Mississippi, 662-453-2239; Thelma's Kitchen, 768 Marietta Street, Atlanta, Georgia, 404-688-5855; and Steins Restaurant, 2248 S. Lauderdale St., Memphis, Tennessee, 901-775-9203.

BALD PEANUTS

Keep your eye out when driving the backroads of the Deep South for roadside shacks with signs advertising "Bald Peanuts." Phonetic for the Southern pronunciation of "boiled peanuts," bald peanuts are a hillbilly hors d'oeuvres par excellence: tender, salty (even spicy), and steaming hot—they're best devoured with an ice-cold RC Cola.

SLEEPS

SHACK UP INN
001 COMMISSARY CIR.
CLARKSDALE, MS
662-624-8329
WWW.SHACKUPINN.COM

A unique B & B—bed & beer, that is—the Shack Up Inn offers authentic shotgun shacks—renovated to have a few

modern conveniences (running water, A/C, kitchens)—that date back to the early twentieth century. These things are the real deal, all weathered Cypress capped with a corrugated tin roof. The proprietors also have an old cotton mill on the property, an old plantation, where they've converted what were once storage bins into overnight accommodations. There's a sporadically open blues club on the premises and plenty more in Clarksdale, just five miles north. The shacks won't set you back much—they start around $50 a night, pillow moon pie included.

AUTHOR'S EPILOGUE

Well, that was that.

Over roughly four months, I drove just over 24,000 miles, only 902 or so short of a lap around the equator. I slept in fifty-four different beds and campsites in that span. I got seven oil changes at four different garages. At one point, I'd been in thirty-five different states in the previous thirty-five days.

There were times that I lamented how many miles and stops and words I had in front of me. I would occasionally lie in bed and wonder how I was going to get all of that traveling and writing done.

That was wrong. Traveling should never be a burden. If it is, it's time to get off the road.

There were also times when I boasted of my rambles. I would throw out impressive numbers like the ones above, telling pretty young girls and cranky old men how much traveling I'd been doing.

That was also wrong. (I'm only bragging again here to make a point.) A wise man told me during my travels that all religions in recorded history have one thing in common: Vanity is no good. In order to move your consciousness to the next level, whatever that level may be, you've got to lose your ego.

"Where does traveling fit into that philosophy?" I asked.

He told me that traveling was its perfect complement. A traveler was a continual stranger seeing new sites with fresh eyes. The rigors of perpetual motion don't meld well with a cumbersome ego. Traveling without might well be the path to enlightenment within, he said—unless, of course, you're bragging about how many miles you've driven, or how many countries you've visited.

Most of all, my rambles were the times of my life. Sasquatch country one week, Yellowstone the next, then Chang and Eng's grave, the Trinity Site, Graceland, and on and on and on. In retrospect, it plays out in my mind like a series of interconnected dreams.

My goal from the get-go was to write about my travels based on six different themes I saw as American archetypes that left lasting cultural marks—like the circus sideshow and the threat of nuclear annihilation.

As my rambles progressed, I was struck by how intertwined my seemingly disparate themes actually were. Bigfoot was the unknown inside of man, the UFOs were the unknown *out there*—the opposite end of the same spectrum. Elvis and alien fanatics seemed as if they belonged to different sects of the same religion. Sin and salvation intersected with the atomic vacation somewhere in the desert, near where humans became most terrifyingly godlike by inventing the atomic bomb. Elvis went to Vegas, I went to Vegas.

So there you have it. I hope my rambles capture the spirit of my favorite country in the world.

RAMBLE MANIFESTO, NOTES

From the second I wake, the pull is strong. My soul once again demands motion. I've slept in the same bed every night for nine weeks or so, about sixty sleeps in all. It's time to go.

At some point in recent memory, I was just as ready for home as I am now ready for the road. Before this homebound stint, I'd been on the road for the better part of two months, driving from the West Texas badlands to the Rockies to Venice Beach, California. Cut to the present: I've only ventured more than fifty miles from home a couple of times in the sixty days since.

All of that stability adds up. I've been sitting too still for too long. The coffee isn't helping quell my nomadic impulses, to be sure, instead fueling the restlessness building in the pit of my gut. Day after day, the feeling has gotten stronger and stronger and by now I've convinced myself the only cure is the road. Regardless of my diagnostic accuracy, I go through the rituals of preparation. I pack a bag of clothes, a smaller bag of toiletries, a backpack, a camera bag, and assorted other bags of various sizes.

I get up early. I load my car. I fill my travel mug with coffee. I double-check everything. I say goodbye to the dog and leave a key under the mat.

Then I go. After a passing thought regarding the position of the coffeemaker's power switch, I recline into my new role. Roles, actually: driver, traveler, nomad. A man going on a journey, a stranger coming to town.

That first morning, that's the road trip big bang, where it all begins. What happened before departure is no longer relevant. Home and bills and jobs and everything else in the rear-view mirror can wait. There is no better diversion from reality than the road.

Home is yin to the road's yang. The conceptual schism between the two is akin to that of the mind's left and right hemispheres, or that of order and chaos. You can't have one without the other. Home is static, stable, and studied—I know most every corner and get more intimate with the place as the clock ticks ahead. Surprises are few, but comforts are many. But you can get too comfortable. Such is the hazard of home.

The road, conversely, is impossible to know like home. Each bend holds the promise of the new, the unique, the unknown. Habit and routine take a backseat to the buzz of discovery, as mile markers and thoughts of all kinds punctuate the long distances driven.

You can get too precise in your daily routine. You can only gargle your name-brand mouthwash for exactly sixty seconds so many times before you want to kick the day-to-day to the curb. Waking leads to coffee which leads to work to lunch to a workout or a daily application of facial cleanser or TV programming or prescription medication. Routine overwhelms everything else; you can actually feel habits cementing into timeworn modes of thought and existence that will be nearly impossible to change. Which brings us back to the relative chaos of the road. The opiate of perpetual motion can salve a soul.

It might sound like I want to take a vacation from myself. It's not entirely untrue. Then there is also the thought that external motion can provoke internal discovery. Life is a journey, and the road trip is a microcosmic symbol of the mortal trek toward enlightenment. Whatever.

My personal angle stems from the desire for a superlative freedom, for those intangible sensations that start in my guts and oscillate along the very center of my being. It's hard to get such primeval juices flowing from the comfort of a sofa, the gentle refrains of TV ads selling your soul into submission. But that's where these words are spilling out of my pen—a cozy dining table in a living room—as my right leg twitches, the rubber on the tip of my tennis shoe squeaking softly on the hardwood. Sure, home is nice. Home is where the heart is. Home sweet home. There's no place like home.

But there's no place like the road either. The predictability of home ultimately fuels the urge to roam. Then there's that burning desire to simply move. There's an allure to velocity that only velocity can placate.

There is nothing in life quite like cruising into a classic Western landscape, radio all the way up, windows all the way down, the sunshine and the beauty and the velocity! Velocity is all-important. Without movement, the road ceases to be. Velocity is the road.

The road calls, and I must listen. And why not? It beats sitting around at home all to hell.

The American road is an endless strip of neon-lit blacktop, lined with billboards, cactus, mountains, urban sprawl, toxic waste, and open space, at once desolate and inspiring and lonely and alive.

The road is also a temporary, ephemeral place. It pulses with activity with or without me, as life stories zoom by at eighty miles an hour. Motion is the norm; to move is to exist. The lack of motion is met with puzzlement and suspicion. Stopping is not a legitimate option.

I drive for hours in a meditative state. Then I think, "Well, I wonder what it's like to live here." At some point, I realized that just about every last spot on the planet was home to somebody. It's the same old shit to somebody. What exactly the same old shit is depends on geography, but it is everywhere.

Except the road. Those fleeting periods of velocity are some of the purest feelings of freedom available. The road is just the place to get lost. And in my mind, that's a good thing.

Caffeine and long-distance driving are inseparable to me. Without coffee, it's doubtful I'd make it very far, mentally or physically. A cup of joe is the ignition for my imagination and inspiration.

I typically refill my travel mug every time I stop. If I chug sixteen ounces of coffee per tank of gas, there is very little chance I'll snooze. Between the caffeine and the sheer volume of fluid, my mind and bladder work hand in hand to keep me awake.

Another essential: music. Beauty is in the ear of the beholder, but the first rule of the road is that you can never have too much music. On a 5,000-mile journey, you could easily listen to 100 different albums and not repeat once. For those types of trips, a serious library is required. Or a well-stocked iPod.

I don't want to dawdle, but I don't want to rush either. Roadside motels are fine en route, but there better be something better at the end of the line. Greasy spoons provide sustenance, but it's best to have sandwich supplies and a steady stream of hot coffee.

Habit can evolve into a near-science. Then I beg for a change, the phone to ring, an email to arrive, anything … .

But nothing happens. And it won't, not unless I can will it so. And the confines of routine cannot involve driving halfway across the country, unless you drive a large vehicle for a living. To make it happen, I must go.

But the wise traveler prepares. There are certain necessities. Clothes, and an organizational system for clean clothes, dirty clothes, and those clothes in between. That usually involves a large mothership bag that remains in the trunk, a satellite bag to bring toiletries and a change into motel rooms and friends' places, and a third bag for the stuff that's in need of a wash.

A full array of camping equipment is another must-have, to shave the lodging costs down and give opportunity to park the car and venture into the woods for a day or three.

Then there's the cooler, which sits in the back seat and occasionally hosts soft drinks and sandwich ingredients. Ice is kept to a minimum.

There's a backpack filled with books and notepads and pens and the like in the front seat and an assortment of CDs with jazz, punk, and country songs. There's a laptop and a camera in the back.

Then there are the little things that suit one's tastes, maybe breath mints, drinking water, and marijuana ... just don't get caught in the red states.

If you leave at the crack of dawn, it is an incredible feeling to rub your eyes at nine o'clock and realize you are nearly 300 miles from home. It would take the pioneers weeks to make it this far. St. Louis to San Francisco was once a harrowing four-month journey. Today it's easy enough to do it in two days.

But the comfort of the couch and the mind-jelling television and the worn pathways of routine, the guaranteed paychecks and the fifteen-minute breaks, it can coalesce into a prison. The only escape is the road.

INDEX

Winchester Mystery House (San Jose, CA): 11
Wolfman Jack: 105
World's Largest Thermometer (Baker, CA): 2
Yosemite Bug (Midpines, CA): 12

PHOTO CREDITS

Dog Bark Park Inn B&B: 43
Friends of Carhenge: 126
Greg Feldman: x
iStockphoto for images from istockphoto.com: 4, 6, 9
Noah Mather: 71
Archie McPhee: 39
Jim Norris: 34
Illustrations by Jaimie Smith, inked by Pan Smith: 27, 119
Shutter Stock for images from shutterstock.com: xiv, 7, 14, 26, 28,
         29, 40, 44, 53, 56, 57, 72, 92, 93, 103, 104, 106, 115, 117, 120,
         121, 122, 131, 136, 138, 141, 154, 155, 174, 175, 169, 171, 189,
         191, 203, 207, 210, 213, and cover
Strangers at the bar: 116
Visit Lubbock: 98
Voodoo Doughnut: 40
Winchester Mystery House: 11

All other photos by Eric Peterson

Maps courtesy of Microsoft®
Streets & Trips 2006 with GPS Locator
www.microsoft.com/streets